Liberia

Liberia

BY RUTH BJORKLUND

Enchantment of the World™
Second Series

CHILDREN'S PRESS®

An Imprint of Scholastic Inc.

Frontispiece: **Mangroves**

Consultant: Cynthia Schmidt, Independent Consultant on African Cultures
Please note: All statistics are as up-to-date as possible at the time of publication.

Book production by The Design Lab

Library of Congress Cataloging-in-Publication Data
Bjorklund, Ruth.
  Liberia / by Ruth Bjorklund.
      pages cm. — (Enchantment of the world)
  Includes bibliographical references and index.
  Audience: Grades 4–6.
  ISBN 978-0-531-21695-8 (library binding : alk. paper)
1. Liberia—Juvenile literature. I. Title.
  DT624.B57 2015
  966.62—dc23   2014048005

1 2 3 4 5 6 7 8 9 10 R 25 24 23 22 21 20 19 18 17 16

Liberian woman

Contents

Left to right: **Dancing, Gbanga, kapok tree, friends, rural house**

CHAPTER 1

Darkness to Dawn

After nine years of the bloody First Liberian Civil War, there was finally a truce in 1997. The only man powerful enough to end the horrible fighting had been elected Liberia's leader. When it was announced that Charles Taylor had won the election, Michael was in school. He was fortunate that his parents could afford school fees, and he was even more fortunate that his school was still standing.

The war had devastated the West African nation of Liberia. Few buildings survived the war. Many homes were reduced to rubble, and many more were vacant, as people had fled Monrovia, the capital, in fear for their lives. Michael's school was a small building made of concrete blocks with a rusted tin roof. Windows had no glass and were placed high on the walls to keep the rain out. But school was a privilege, and the brightly painted classroom walls and worn, donated schoolbooks were a treasure.

Michael's father worked for the government. Before the war, they lived in a suburb of small concrete homes, lush gardens, and muddy unpaved streets. Some people had electricity

Opposite: **A teacher giving Liberian children a lesson in math. The nation's long periods of civil war disrupted the education of many children.**

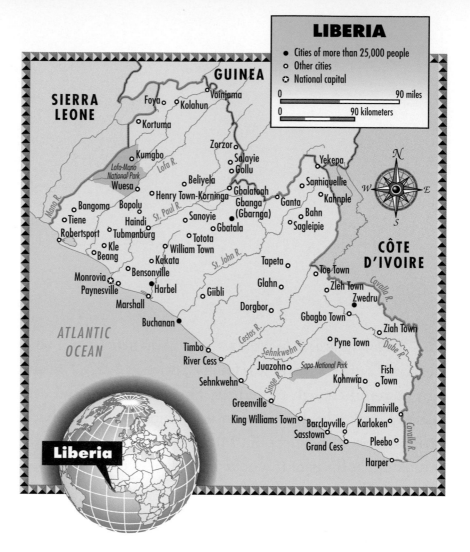

in his neighborhood, but not all. His family had a gas-powered generator to run the refrigerator and charge their cell phones. But everyone had running water, unlike many other neighborhoods near Monrovia.

Charles Taylor was not a peaceful man. He was a violent warlord, but he had been elected because he promised to stop the fighting. But peace did not last, and new rebel armies began attacking villages and towns in 1999, starting the Second Liberian Civil War. Eventually, the armies moved into

Monrovia. Government buildings and entire neighborhoods were bombed. People took shelter in abandoned office buildings, theaters, and libraries.

Wealthy people, businesspeople, and those with relatives in other countries were able to flee the country by airplane or ship. Other people had no easy way to leave. The railways had been destroyed in the first civil war. Few people had cars. It was the rainy season and all the roads leading out of Monrovia were muddy with deep potholes and mountains of debris. The poor and less fortunate packed what belongings they could and walked for weeks through the rain forest to cross the border into Sierra Leone or Côte d'Ivoire.

Warlord Charles Taylor holds a gun aloft during the First Liberian Civil War. Taylor fought rival groups for eight years and later became president.

Michael's father knew they would not be safe in Monrovia. The family did not have enough money for an airline ticket or a ship's boarding pass. They had no car. So they packed their belongings—a few clothes, a cook pot, a knife, a shovel, bags of rice, and a hunting rifle—and set out.

Michael and his family headed toward the highlands. They hiked through the rain forest and foraged for food, finding fruits such as coconuts, bananas, and papayas. Michael's father sometimes shot a bat or a monkey to eat. Michael and his younger sister collected wood and his mother made charcoal. They dug a pit and set the wood on fire, and then pounded

A girl peels a mango, one of the many fruits that grow well in Liberia.

A boy plays a drum at the Buduburam refugee camp. Liberians continued to live at the camp a decade after the second civil war ended.

it until hard pieces of charcoal formed. The charcoal burned hotter and it was easier to carry than wood.

After several weeks, Michael and his family reached the border of Ghana. They were destined for a refugee camp called Buduburam. Thousands of Liberian refugees lived in Buduburam. Michael met many interesting people at the camp, including Liberians from other cities and towns and from tiny villages deep in the forest, as well as aid workers from foreign countries.

For the first three years of the first civil war, the refugees had lived in tents with little water, but by the time Michael's family came nine years later, international organizations had helped build small houses, shops, and health clinics. There was even electricity, drinking water, and, to Michael's astonishment, schools.

Liberians scatter as a mortar shell explodes in Monrovia in 2003. At least 150,000 people were killed during Liberia's civil wars.

Back in Liberia, the second civil war raged on, fiercer and bloodier than the first civil war. More people streamed in across the border from Liberia looking for safety at Buduburam. In 2003, the refugees got word that Charles Taylor had left the country and that a temporary government was in place.

There was so much destruction at home in Liberia, but still Michael was eager to go back. He had gone to junior high school at the camp, but hoped to finish senior high school in Monrovia.

When Michael and his family returned to their old neighborhood, they were overwhelmed by the destruction and the crumbled buildings and looted homes. It was a huge undertaking, but Michael and his family and neighbors began to rebuild. The family did not have any money left for school fees so Michael did not go back to school. But he found many jobs working in construction.

In 2014, Michael read a newspaper article in the *Monrovia Daily Observer*. It was about a boy who had grown up in the Buduburam refugee camp. His father had started a children's tennis academy there. With an amazing amount of determination and faith in himself, Alfred Saah Kandakai, at age fourteen, was training in the United States and representing Liberia in international junior tennis tournaments. Michael felt such pride. The boy, raised in a refugee camp and a citizen of one of the poorest nations in the world, had found the strength in himself to pursue his dreams. Michael has faith that all Liberians will find that same strength to survive, rebuild, and achieve.

The word *hope* is painted on a building in Monrovia. Liberians remain hopeful that the bloody strife of the nation's past will not return.

CHAPTER 2

Land of Beauty

T HE FIRST WOMAN ELECTED PRESIDENT IN ALL OF Africa, Ellen Johnson Sirleaf described her homeland of Liberia as "a beautiful, mixed-up country struggling mightily to find itself." Liberia has a warm, tropical climate; abundant rainfall; glistening ocean beaches; fertile farmland; and lush rain forests. Yet some of its beauty and natural resources have been marred by environmental damage and decades of devastating war.

Opposite: **Sandy beaches line much of the Liberian coast.**

A West African Land

Liberia lies on the coast of West Africa. Covering 38,250 square miles (99,067 square kilometers), Liberia is similar in size to the U.S. state of Virginia. Sierra Leone borders Liberia to the northwest. Guinea lies northeast of Liberia. Côte d'Ivoire (Ivory Coast) forms an eastern border. The Atlantic Ocean is Liberia's southern border. The country is an irregularly shaped rectangle. At its widest, it is 148 miles (238 kilometers), and at its longest, 142 miles (229 km).

Liberia has four main geographical regions: the coast, rolling hills, the plateau, and the highlands. The Atlantic coastline is relatively unbroken, but for a few sandbars, artificial harbors, and rocky outcroppings, such as Cape Palmas near the Côte d'Ivoire border and Cape Mount on the northwest border. The coastline's long, sandy beaches give way to flat coastal plains made up of lagoons and mangrove swamps. Beyond is a wide swath of gently rolling hills, covered in heavy grasses, thick shrubs, and leafy trees. The central and southeastern region forms a plateau with elevations of 600 to 900 feet (180 to 270 meters). It is the largest geographic area in the country, and it

A wooden bridge crosses a river near the border with Sierra Leone, where the land is covered with thick bushes.

The Freeport of Monrovia

Monrovia's harbor, called the Freeport of Monrovia, is one of the most famous seaports in the world. In the nineteenth and early twentieth centuries, it was a small, shallow port in the Mesurado River and only small ships could anchor there. In 1942, Liberia entered World War II on the side of the United States and its allies. The United States was manufacturing airplanes and vehicles and needed rubber. Liberia could supply rubber, but it had no means of loading large quantities of rubber onto ships. To maintain an uninterrupted supply of rubber, American troops landed in Liberia and improved the port. By 1948, after the war had ended, soldiers had created a huge deepwater harbor. Today, other artificial harbors have changed Liberia's coastline in sites such as Greenville, Harper, and Buchanan.

is where the densest rain forests are found. In the northwest is a section of the Guinea Highlands, which extend into Guinea and Côte d'Ivoire. There are several mountain ranges, including the Putu, Bong, Wologizi, and Nimba ranges. Liberia's tallest peak is Mount Wuteve, which rises 4,724 feet (1,440 m) above sea level and is located in the Wologizi Range.

Rivers, Lakes, and the Sea

There are fifteen major rivers in Liberia, and all flow into the Atlantic Ocean. In the north, the Mano, joined by the Mauwa, Magowi, and Morro, separate Liberia from Sierra Leone and parts of Guinea. The longest river, the Cavalla, flows for 320 miles (515 km) and forms Liberia's border with

A woman rows down the Du River in northern Liberia. In many parts of Liberia, traveling by boat is the easiest way to get around.

Côte d'Ivoire. There are four other main rivers, the Lofa, Cestos, Saint Paul, and Saint John. The larger rivers flow down from the mountains in Guinea. The smaller rivers rise from the Liberian highlands. Filled with rapids, narrow channels, waterfalls, sandbars, and small islands, the rivers are not easily navigated by anything but small boats and dugout canoes. Where the rivers empty into the ocean they create lagoons and estuaries—a mixture of saltwater and freshwater.

The Atlantic Ocean is shallow as it reaches shore. While beachgoers have numerous beaches to choose from, many are too dangerous for swimming. The most famous beaches are those around Robertsport near Cape Mount, where Liberians and people from around the world come to surf.

The nation's largest lake, Lake Piso, also called Fisherman's Lake, is located in the northwest of the country. It covers an area of nearly 40 square miles (100 sq km). Three rivers empty into the lake, and because there is an open channel leading into the Atlantic Ocean, the lake is salty. After heavy rains fell in 1998, the lake burst its banks, flooding nineteen surrounding villages and leaving more than two thousand people homeless. Lake Shepard, a large lake in the south, is calm and peaceful, and residents find it a refreshing destination to picnic and swim. Deep inside the forest in Bong County, east of Monrovia, are many waterfalls, including Kpatawee Falls, a large, three-tiered waterfall that races down from the hills.

Refreshing Kpatawee Falls lies hidden in the forest.

The Mystery of Blue Lake

In the late 1960s and early 1970s, a Liberian iron ore mining company operated in the Bomi Hills north of Monrovia. Heavy mining equipment dug immense holes in the earth. When the company abandoned its mines, the region was scarred with giant, unsightly craters. Curiously, years later, one of the craters filled with water. The source of the water is unknown—no springs, creeks, or rivers seem to feed the lake. It is a crystal-clear blue lake, which gives it its name, Blue Lake. The lake teems with fish. The water is so pure that there is a mineral water bottling plant along the lake's shore.

In the Tropics

Liberia is located near the equator, an imaginary line that runs around the globe an equal distance between the North and the South Poles. This gives Liberia a tropical climate that is warm year-round. The average high temperature in July is 84 degrees Fahrenheit (29 degrees Celsius) and the average high temperature in January is 88°F (31°C).

Liberia has definite seasons, but only two—a dry season and a rainy season. The rainy season begins in April or May and ends in October or November. The capital city of Monrovia receives about 202 inches (514 centimeters) of rain a year, making it the rainiest capital city in the world. The heavy rainfall swamps roadways and houses. Rivers flood their banks. The humidity is extremely high, and very few buildings have air-conditioning. Often, schools will close when the weather is extremely hot, humid, and uncomfortable. People stay indoors as much as they can. There is sometimes a slight

Liberia's Geographic Features

Area: 38,250 square miles (99,067 sq km)

Length of Coastline: 359 miles (578 km)

Highest Elevation: Mount Wuteve, 4,724 feet (1,440 m) above sea level

Lowest Elevation: Sea level along the coast

Widest Point East to West: 148 miles (238 km)

Widest Point North to South: 142 miles (229 km)

Longest River: Cavalla, 320 miles (515 km)

Average High Temperature: In Monrovia, 88°F (31°C) in January, 84°F (29°C) in July

Average Low Temperature: In Monrovia, 70°F (21°C) in January, 70°F (21°C) in July

Average Ocean Temperature: 81°F (27°C)

Average Annual Precipitation: 202 inches (514 cm) in Monrovia

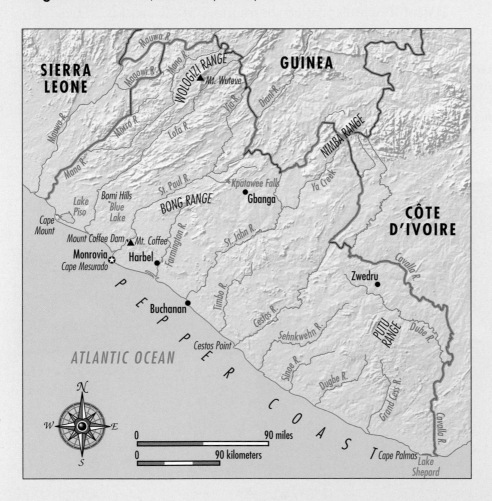

break in the heat for a couple of weeks in late July and early August. Liberians call the break the "middle dries."

Winter is the dry season. Liberians often say that they are fortunate that they never experience natural disasters—no earthquakes, tornadoes, hurricanes, or tidal waves strike their country. However, winter does bring harsh and sometimes harmful winds, called harmattan trade winds. These hot, dusty winds howl down from the Sahara, a massive desert that stretches across North Africa, and whip up dust and debris. Airplanes are sometimes grounded because of the swirling sands. People must wear protective clothing to keep from being pelted by particles in the wind.

A woman removes water from her flooded home near Monrovia, where flooding is common in the summer months.

A Look at Liberia's Cities

The capital city of Monrovia is by far the largest city in the country, with a population of more than 1 million. Liberia's second-largest city, Gbanga (or Gbarnga, below), has more than 330,000 residents. It is the only major city that is located inland rather than on the coast. It is surrounded by forests and farms, with Kpatawee Falls nearby. Gbanga is a regional center for trade and manufacturing, and is the home of the Kpelle, the largest Liberian ethnic group. Just outside the city is the main campus of Cuttington University, founded in 1889 by the Episcopal Church of the United States.

Buchanan (right) is the third-largest city, with about 50,000 people. It is located on the coast along the

St. John River, and was founded by African American Quakers from Pennsylvania in 1835. It was named after President James Buchanan's brother, who was Liberia's first governor. The earliest residents were an indigenous people called the Bassa, who continue to reside in the area. As a result, many people refer to the city as Grand Bassa. In 1968, an artificial deepwater port was completed in Buchanan. It is the country's second-largest port.

Harbel lies along the Farmington River, about 32 miles (51 km) from the Freeport of Monrovia. In 1926, the Firestone Tire and Rubber Company established a vast rubber tree plantation and manufacturing complex there. Harbel was named for the founder of the company and his wife, Harvey and Idabelle Firestone. Both Harbel and the inland city of Zwedru are home to about 25,000 people.

CHAPTER 3

A Biodiversity Hot Spot

PLANTS AND ANIMALS THRIVE IN LIBERIA'S HOT, wet climate. The country's tropical forests make up one of only thirty-five areas in the world labeled a "global biodiversity hot spot." The term refers to any geographic region that contains biologically rare and important plants and animals and whose habitat is threatened with destruction. Biodiversity hot spots cover only about 2 percent of the world's surface but support nearly 60 percent of the world's plant, bird, mammal, reptile, and amphibian species.

Rain forest covers more than 40 percent of Liberia, but the forests are under threat. Logging companies, many of them illegal, have been cutting and exporting thousands of acres of rain forest hardwood, such as mahogany, ironwood, and teak. Mining operations damage forests when they scour mountainsides digging for ore. Liberian farmers contribute

Opposite: **Liberia's Nimba Range has extraordinary biodiversity. The mountains are home to more than a hundred kinds of mammals and thousands of other species, many of which live nowhere else.**

to the destruction by burning forests to make way for new fields. Still, Liberia has one of the last major tracts of rain forest in all of West Africa. In a recent count, the forests are home to 2,200 species of plants, 193 mammal species, and 576 bird species, creating one of the world's greatest regions of biodiversity. New efforts are being made by government and international environmental groups to preserve Liberia's valuable forests. During a meeting on world climate held at the United Nations in 2014, the country of Norway offered to pay Liberia to stop cutting down its forests.

Large swaths of Liberian rain forest have been cut down to make room for farms.

Sapo National Park

Sapo National Park, along the Sinoe River in south-eastern Liberia, was established in 1982, becoming Liberia's first national park. The park features a mixture of rain forest, swamps, and grasslands along with the foothills of the Putu Mountains. The forests of the park have never been logged, which makes it West Africa's largest intact rain forest. Sapo National Park is home to an enormous variety of plants and animals, including the forest elephant, the zebra duiker (left), and the rare pygmy hippopotamus. The rangers do their best to protect the animals. They have installed hidden cameras around the park to monitor for hunters. Visiting the park is difficult as there are no roads or public hiking trails inside the park.

Along the Coast

Different types of plants grow in Liberia's variety of landscapes. Coastal plants include many grasses and small bushes that hold down the soil and prevent erosion by the ocean's waves and powerful winds. Mangrove forests are also vital to the preservation of Liberia's coastline. Mangroves grow in shallow tidal water. Their roots grow down from their branches to form a tangled root-ball that rises above the water. When the tide rushes in, it swamps the roots. When it flows out, the roots catch mud and debris, eventually forming land. The trees form a barrier that protects the shoreline from storms and are a rich habitat for a wide variety of plant and animal life, such as wading birds, fish, lobsters, crabs, and crocodiles.

Standing Tall

The kapok tree, also known as ceiba, and called *ghé* in Liberia, can live for one thousand years if it is left to grow. The kapok needs a large amount of sunlight and grows rapidly, often as much as 13 feet (4 m) a year, in order to stand above the surrounding forest. Once the tree reaches full height—sometimes up to 200 feet (60 m)—it spreads its branches outward. These trees provide a habitat for birds, frogs, insects, bats, and monkeys. The kapok tree is often found in moist rain forest. In the rainy season, the tree's leaves grow bright green, long, and waxy, and in the dry season they drop off. Small peach flowers form, followed by a long pod. When the pod ripens and falls, puffy, violet-colored balls of fiber remain on the bare branches. The fiber is commonly called kapok. It floats, is resistant to moisture, and is often used in making life vests. Kapok has also been used to stuff pillows and mattresses.

Rain Forests

Some of Liberia's rain forest is semi-deciduous, meaning that some of the trees lose their leaves. Much of the semi-deciduous rain forest lies in the northern half of the country. The evergreen rain forest covers eastern and southeastern Liberia. Highly prized rain forest trees include rosewood, ironwood, walnut, teak, mahogany, and ebony. Baobab, African oak, kola, and oil palms are also common. Among the many native tree and plant species are some that are also grown commercially, including coffee, rubber, cacao, raffia palms, oil palms, and pineapple.

The semi-deciduous rain forests occur where the dry and rainy seasons are more pronounced. Those forests are less dense than the evergreen forests. The evergreen rain forests do not experience a very long dry season so the trees do not shed their leaves. Evergreen rain forest trees grow very close to one another. In order to survive, each tree must be exposed to sunlight. So trees grow straight and tall and do not branch out until they reach the forest canopy, or treetops.

A man works on a rubber plantation in Kakata, east of Monrovia. Rubber is made from the sap of the tree, which flows when the bark is removed.

Many species of vines, ferns, creepers, and lianas are found in the rain forest. Ferns and creepers grow on the forest floor and can grow in low light. But vines and lianas need sunlight. They root in the ground and use the trees for support, sending out little roots into the bark as they grow toward the top of the canopy. Vines are relatively harmless plants, but lianas can be thick and woody. Lianas weave through the canopy, connecting trees together. Monkeys and chimpanzees use them to swing from branch to branch, but many lianas, such as the strangling fig, damage trees.

Liberia has one of the largest chimpanzee populations in West Africa. The nation is home to about seven thousand chimpanzees.

The pink trumpet vine produces many delicate pink flowers.

Bursts of Color

Flowers are a spectacular part of Liberia's landscape. Whether growing on the ground like the blue sky flower or on a bush such as a wild gardenia or a pink trumpet creeper, the colors and aromas of Liberia's flowers are stunning. Because of the country's plentiful sun and rain, flowers are not held to a single growing season, so blooms are abundant year-round. The rain forest is home to a wide variety of flowers. Many of them are epiphytic, meaning that they grow attached to other plants and trees. Some ferns and mosses are epiphytic, as are the hundreds of species of colorful and sweet-smelling orchids.

The Pepper Coast

In the sixteenth century, Portuguese sailors were among the first European traders along the West African coast. They named the various coastlines after the trade goods they collected. Present day Ghana was called the Gold Coast until 1957, and Liberia's neighbor is still called Côte d'Ivoire (Ivory Coast). Before Liberia was established in 1821, it was known as the Grain Coast or the Pepper Coast, after the spicy Melegueta pepper. The pepper is found throughout Liberia's coastal areas and it is the national flower. Traditionally used in cooking, the pepper was also used to make medicines and fabric dyes. The plant has a sweet, spicy smell. The seeds of the Melegueta pepper, so highly prized in cooking, are called Grains of Paradise.

In the Air

With its diversity of landscapes, from woodlands to grasslands to rain forest, Liberia supports a staggering variety of animal species. Many of the birds found in Liberia live in the country year-round. Other birds migrate. Some raise their young in Liberia, while others simply stop off there while escaping cold winters elsewhere. Common birds include woodpeckers, parrots, doves, and sparrows. In the wetlands are wading birds such as flamingos, storks, herons, egrets, spoonbills, and plovers. The white-breasted guinea fowl and the Liberian black flycatcher are rare. The country is home to many seabirds, including frigate birds, gulls, and pelicans. There are also many birds of prey, such as African harrier hawks, crowned eagles, and martial eagles. Crowned eagles and other birds that hunt in the rain forest attack their prey from

below, flying upward to overpower bats, birds, squirrels, sloths, and monkeys. The martial eagle is Liberia's largest eagle with a wingspan nearly 100 inches (250 cm) across. It can tackle and kill an antelope five times its weight.

Bats and insects make up the other creatures of the air. Bats, the only flying mammal, make up 20 percent of all Liberia's mammal species. As nocturnal hunters, they feed at night and hang upside down in caves, crevices, and trees during the day. Different bat species have different diets. Some eat fruit and nectar, while others eat small mammals, birds, lizards, frogs, and fish.

Liberians know to be wary of mosquitoes, which can carry dangerous diseases such as yellow fever, dengue fever, and malaria, and tsetse flies, which can induce "sleeping sickness." They are also careful where they step, in order to avoid termites, poisonous spiders, scorpions, and fire ants or red ants, which have a painful sting.

There are many harmless insects, including wasps, honeybees, dragonflies, butterflies, moths, and grasshoppers. In 2009, and again in 2014, northeastern Liberia was overrun by tens of millions of caterpillars. They descended on more than fifty villages, devouring crops.

Reptiles and Amphibians

Reptiles and amphibians are found throughout Liberia. Reptiles include lizards such as geckos and chameleons, as well as the West African dwarf crocodile, a creature that can live as long as one hundred years. Endangered loggerhead sea turtles live off the coast and lay their eggs on the beaches.

Approximately seventy species of snakes live in Liberia. Most are harmless, but a few can be deadly. Bush vipers and rhinoceros vipers live on the rain forest floor and attack prey with venomous folding fangs. Black mamba snakes hunt on the ground but are able to easily scale trees in search of prey. Green mambas hide in tree branches and wait for prey. The

The eyes and nostrils of the West African dwarf crocodile are located on top of its head. This allows it to hide quietly in the water and yet still breathe and watch until prey comes by.

green mamba's jaw dislocates so that it can swallow an animal up to four times the size of its head. Liberia is also home to asps, boa constrictors, cobras, and adders. One of the most unusual frogs is the shy goliath frog, which reaches a length of 3 feet (90 cm).

The goliath frog feeds on worms, insects, smaller frogs, and small reptiles.

Water Dwellers

There are more than five hundred species of freshwater fish in Liberia's rivers and lakes. They range from small, brightly colored tetra fish to large African catfish. There are also elephant fish, trunkfish, and tilapia, which is a staple in many Liberians' diet. Large marine fish such as blue marlin, yellowfin tuna, and sailfish swim in a deep trench off the coast.

Manatees, shy marine mammals also called sea cows, glide silently in the calm waters of the mangrove swamps. Dolphins and whales live along the coast.

Mammals

The diversity of mammals in Liberia is impressive. Animals ranging in Liberia's grasslands and forests include leopards, servals, civets, mongooses, wild hogs, warthogs, badgers, linsangs, porcupines, polecats, and pangolins. Antelopes, such as duikers and bushbucks, as well as many species of monkeys and chimpanzees also inhabit the land.

Liberia has been stricken with years of war, and many species have lost their habitat to fighting, logging, and over-hunting. Some creatures that were once common in the region are now rarely, if ever, sighted, including the African lion, the African buffalo, and the Cross River gorilla, the most endangered gorilla species in the world. West Africa's forest elephant is a secretive animal that lives in the dense rain forest. It is smaller than a savanna elephant and its tusks grow downward, rather than out. Before war overtook the country, Liberia was home to more than twenty thousand forest elephants, but now fewer than one thousand remain. They have been hunted for ivory and for meat.

Liberia's forests are also home to many endangered animals. The western red colobus monkey and the Diana monkey are both in danger of extinction. Western red colobus monkeys are very social creatures that live in groups high in the rain forest canopy. They have long red fur on their heads and shoulders, and tails that reach lengths of 2 feet (60 cm). The long fur acts as a parachute when they fling themselves from branch to branch. Liberia is also home to the rare Jentink's duiker and zebra duiker. These tiny antelopes are extremely shy. In fact, their name *duiker* comes from a word meaning "diving buck," because of their habit of diving into the forest or under cover at the first sign of an intruder.

Wet and Wild

The pygmy hippopotamus is about one-quarter the size of a full-size hippopotamus. Pygmy hippos are a distant relative of the whale and spend most of their time in water to keep their skin wet and their body temperature cool. Only about two thousand pygmy hippos remain in the world, and nearly all live in Liberia near Sapo National Park. Pygmy hippos are secretive and peaceful. They eat ferns, leaves, and grasses, mostly at night.

CHAPTER 4

The First People

THE FIRST HUMANS TO WALK THE EARTH LIVED ON the continent of Africa. As human society developed, some groups migrated to other areas, seeking new sources of food or better living conditions. It is not clear who the first people were to migrate to the area that is now called Liberia. But legends and oral histories of many groups say these people were small in size. Liberian historian Abayomi Karnga described them as people who "dwelt in caves and the hollows of large trees, and lived on fruits and roots of wild trees."

Opposite: **A mask from Liberia's Gio culture. Such masks are worn at ceremonies and performances.**

The Sixteen Ethnic Groups of Liberia

Between the eleventh and seventeenth centuries, the ancestors of what are known as the sixteen Liberian indigenous (native-born) groups migrated into West Africa. Many had lived near the Sahara, where shifting sands overtook their farms and villages. West Africa's rain forests provided not only fertile

farmland but also an abundance of animals to hunt. Others fled from invaders who came from the east and the north of Africa. The larger indigenous groups then separated into smaller, related ethnic groups, referred to locally as "tribes."

The first people were mostly root vegetable farmers from the upper Niger River to the east. Likely the first groups to arrive were the Gola and Kissi peoples, although some historians believe that small groups of Dei people had already settled in Liberia by the time they arrived. The Gola are speakers of the Mel language group.

These first groups were joined by the Kruan-speaking peoples who came from what is now Côte d'Ivoire. They were seafarers and fishers who arrived by boat and settled on the coast. They separated into six ethnic groups—the Bassa, Bella, Dei, Grebo, Krahn, and Kru.

The third major population that settled in Liberia were the Mande-speaking peoples—the Bandi, Kpelle, Loma, Mano, Gio, and Mende. They were from the savanna region and were chiefly farmers but also potters, weavers, blacksmiths, and traders. They fashioned arrowheads, knives, rings, and iron rods, which they used for money.

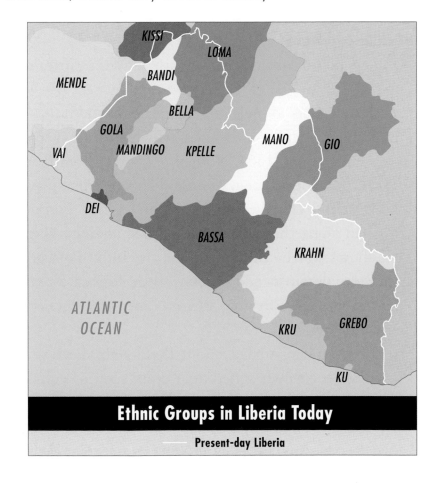

Ethnic Groups in Liberia Today

—— Present-day Liberia

In the sixteenth and seventeenth centuries, the Vai and the Mandingo peoples migrated into the region. After arriving, the Vai clashed with the Golas, defeated them, and settled along the coast near Sierra Leone. The Vai were one of the first groups in Africa to develop a written language. The Mandingo had belonged to the Kingdom of Mali in the western Sudan region to the north. Unlike other groups, the Mandingo did not farm. Instead, they traveled from village to village buying, selling, and trading goods.

Foreign Encounters

Arab traders began visiting inland parts of West Africa and the coast as early as 750 CE. For centuries, they kept ties with West African leaders to trade salt, copper, silk, and horses for gold, ivory, grains, and animal hides, which they then traded to Europeans. Around 1364, Norman explorers from France settled briefly on the Liberian coast and bought ivory, pepper, gold, and African sandalwood. By the mid-1400s, European traders sailed along the coast. The first documented visit to Liberian shores was by the Portuguese. In 1461, Portuguese explorer Pedro de Sintra and his crew made contact for trade with indigenous people in what are now Liberia, Sierra Leone, and Côte d'Ivoire.

The West Africans traded among themselves. Each group of people had their own agricultural crop, such as palm oil or plantains, or their own manufactured item, such as metal tools, pottery, or baskets. Local leaders made certain that the exchange of goods was fair. They also refused to exchange with

Slavery in Africa

For centuries, African and Arab traders included enslaved persons as part of their exchanges. Many of those who were enslaved were prisoners of war in ethnic conflicts, had committed crimes, or owed a debt. Enslaved persons were laborers, household workers, or farmers and were often respected for their abilities. In many situations, enslaved people had the right to marry and to own property. They could sometimes purchase their freedom. Enslavement was also sometimes temporary—people could be freed once they had worked off their punishment or labored to repay a debt. In many ways, the West African system of slavery resembled the European system of indentured servitude rather than the system of slavery that developed in the Americas.

any trader caught cheating or taking advantage of another trader. When the Portuguese first arrived, they raided coastal villages, but they later realized better profits and a variety of goods would come if they traded fairly with the local people. They traded tools, knives, cooking pots, and textiles for ivory, gold, palm oil, and spices. For more than a century, Portuguese traders controlled all trade between Europe and coastal West Africa, and their influence is still evident in the names of rivers, mountains, and other sites. But by the sixteenth century, British, French, Spanish, and Dutch traders had also become frequent visitors.

African captives are brought on board for shipment to the Americas. Although the slave trade was gradually outlawed beginning in the late 1700s, it did not completely end until 1870, when Portugal stopped its last slave trade route to Brazil.

Eve of Destruction

The arrival of the Europeans had a devastating impact on life in Africa. In the sixteenth century, trade increased rapidly between West Africa and Europe and African leaders competed with one another for the opportunity to barter with the Europeans. It was a sign of wealth in West Africa to be a slave owner and so leaders began to offer enslaved people in their trades.

In the meantime, the newly settled colonies in the Americas were rapidly changing. Originally, Europeans had gone to the Americas looking for gold. But later they began producing agricultural crops for export to Europe. Most in demand by Europeans were cotton, tobacco, and sugar, all crops that required grueling labor to produce. At first planters used indentured European servants—people who worked for a few years without pay in exchange for free passage to America. However, more workers were needed.

In Africa, European traders first began capturing coastal people and enslaving them, but before long they began bargaining with African leaders. The slave trade soon began. The trade became profitable for the Europeans as well as the local African leaders. Eventually, the African leaders exhausted their own supply of enslaved people and looked into acquiring more. They sent kidnappers into the interior to bring back young and healthy people. After the kidnappers marched the captured men and women through the forests to the coast, they imprisoned them in crude barracks to wait for the traders to arrive.

As profits from sugar, cotton, and tobacco began to soar, European traders became interested only in the slave trade and no longer paid attention to luxury goods. Likewise, most local leaders preferred to trade for horses, guns, and gunpowder. A vicious cycle began. As the Europeans demanded more slaves, the Africans demanded more guns in order to capture more slaves. In the end, more than fifteen million Africans were captured and enslaved.

The slave trade caused hostility among West African peoples. Various ethnic groups were pitted against one another as kidnapping raids terrorized inland villages. The coastal groups became dominant and more brutal. The cooperative and mutually beneficial trading economy that had once thrived was destroyed.

Distant Changes Afoot

Into the nineteenth century, millions of Africans and their descendants in North America continued to be enslaved. However, there was a small but growing population of Africans who were freed from slavery. Their freedom came in several ways. From April 1775 until December 1783, the American colonies were at war with Britain in a fight for independence. Many slave owners joined the American Patriot army and left their farms and plantations behind. Thousands of enslaved people then escaped. Other enslaved people joined the British to fight their American oppressors. After the war the British freed many, although not all, enslaved soldiers. By the nineteenth century, groups in England and the new United States began demanding an end to slavery. In 1808, Britain officially ended the slave trade.

In the meantime, the northern United States was becoming more urban.

A portrait of Caesar, one of the last slaves in New York. The state began limiting slavery after 1799, but it did not completely abolish it until 1827.

People moved to cities and new industries developed. Many northerners were relying less on free labor. They began freeing their enslaved people, especially those who were older and less able to work. Some northerners also freed the children of their enslaved workers. Some enslaved people were allowed to purchase their freedom or were freed upon the death of an owner. The South, on the other hand, increased its employment of enslaved workers. Southerners also increased purchases before the 1808 deadline, when trade with Britain for slaves would no longer be possible.

A meeting of the American Colonization Society. Its membership was almost entirely white.

In the nineteenth century, several movements to end, or abolish, slavery took hold in the United States. People who wanted an end to slavery were called abolitionists. In 1816, a group made up of a mix of northerners, many of whom were members of a religious group known as the Quakers, and southerners, many of whom were former slaveholders, formed a private organization called the American Colonization Society (ACS). The organization was supported by many well-known American political figures, including Thomas Jefferson, James Madison, and James Monroe. The abolitionists were morally opposed to slavery and believed that free blacks would have a better, safer life in Africa than in the United States. The Quakers also recognized that many American blacks were Christian and saw an opportunity to spread Christianity further in Africa. The slaveholders also wanted to see free blacks move to Africa. They worried that free blacks in the United States would encourage enslaved blacks to revolt. Together these unlikely partners in the ACS raised money to take a group of free black Americans to Africa and create a home for them.

Bittersweet Return

In 1821, the U.S. Congress agreed to support the ACS and granted it $100,000 to finance the trip. Most free black Americans had no interest in going to West Africa. For many, their friends and families had been in the United States for several generations. However, in 1820, eighty-six American blacks volunteered to go along with three white ACS agents. They sailed to West Africa and looked for land to colonize, finally landing at Cape Mesurado on the Liberian coast. The Americans were not well received. The local Dei and Bassa people had every reason to be suspicious. Just fourteen years prior, white men that resembled the ACS agents had been at their shores and raiding their people. Furthermore, the slave trade was still going on

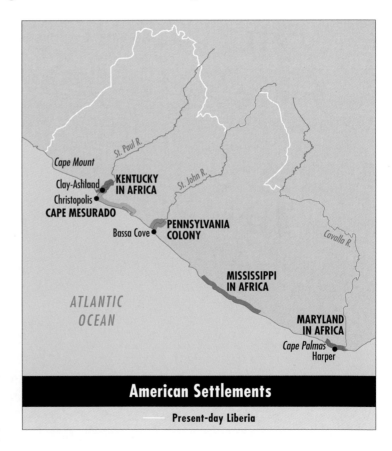

Cape Mount

St. Paul R.

Clay-Ashland
Christopolis
CAPE MESURADO
KENTUCKY
IN AFRICA

St. John R.

Bassa Cove
PENNSYLVANIA
COLONY

Cavalla R.

ATLANTIC
OCEAN

MISSISSIPPI
IN AFRICA

MARYLAND
IN AFRICA

Cape Palmas
Harper

American Settlements
— Present-day Liberia

illegally. The ACS agents had little success in finding anyone to sell them land. Eventually, a Bassa leader, held at gunpoint, agreed to sell the Americans a strip of coastline, 36 miles (58 km) long and 3 miles (5 km) wide, in exchange for six muskets, one barrel of gunpowder, six iron bars, one barrel of rum, and various small items. All told, these items were worth just $300.

On February 6, 1820, the Americans established the first settlement and named their village Christopolis. During the first year of colonization, twenty-two of the eighty-six settlers and all three of the ACS officials died of yellow fever or malaria.

Meanwhile, in the United States, slave-owning states were urging free blacks to leave and resettle in West Africa. They

African Americans board a ship in Savannah, Georgia, to emigrate to Liberia.

Edward Wilmot Blyden (standing, right), a free black man from Saint Thomas, an island in the Caribbean, emigrated to Liberia in 1851 after being refused admission to a college in New Jersey because of his race. In Liberia, he became a prominent teacher, newspaper editor, writer, and, eventually, secretary of state.

founded other societies. Some enslaved blacks were given their freedom only if they agreed to emigrate. The Maryland State Colonization Society established a colony in Cape Palmas, as did Mississippi. The Virginia Colonization Society, the Quaker Young Men's Colonization Society of Pennsylvania, and the American Colonization Society together took control of all settlements between the Cestos River and Cape Mount. Between 1822 and 1867, the ACS groups helped nearly 20,000 people, including 5,700 who were rescued from illegal slave-trading ships, to settle in West Africa. This was just a small percentage of the nearly two million free black people living in the United States at that time.

Going It Alone

Life was difficult for the emigrants. The skills they learned on farms in the United States did not prepare them for farming in Liberia's climate. Tropical diseases took many lives. The indigenous, or native, West Africans disliked the newcomers who were taking over the coastal areas, ending the profitable, but illegal, slave trade, and preaching Christianity. In 1824, the settlement of Christopolis was renamed Monrovia, after U.S. president James Monroe, who had been a supporter of ACS. The collection of settlements was called the colony of Liberia, meaning "land of the free." It was the first permanent black American settlement in West Africa.

The U.S. Congress never established Liberia as an official American colony. The country is, in fact, one of only two African countries that were never colonized by another nation. The downside of not being a colony was that the United States was never obligated to protect Liberia from outside forces. During the 1830s, Liberia's neighbors were colonized by the British (Sierra Leone) and the French (Guinea, Côte d'Ivoire), taking over lands Liberians had previously claimed. The United States did nothing to assist the Liberians. In the 1840s, the ACS ran out of money and wanted to end its commitment to Liberia and asked Liberia to claim independence.

In 1847, eleven Liberian delegates met and decided that Liberia would become an independent nation named the Republic of Liberia. It would be the oldest black republic in Africa. They wrote a constitution that was based on the U.S. Constitution. The Liberian constitution granted all former enslaved people and their descendants full rights of citizenship. However, the constitution denied those rights to the indigenous Liberians, who were not allowed to own property or vote. Liberia's first president, Joseph Jenkins Roberts, visited foreign rulers and asked them to recognize Liberia's independence. Great Britain recognized Liberia as an independent country in 1848, and Germany, France, Portugal, Austria, Brazil, Norway, and Sweden soon followed. Not until 1862 did the United States, under President Abraham Lincoln, recognize the Republic of Liberia as an independent nation.

Monrovia was a growing town in the 1850s.

Building a Nation

After Liberia became independent, Roberts worked to expand the country's borders. He sent troops to outlying settlements to fight indigenous groups that resisted the new government. He signed treaties with local political leaders and purchased land so that by 1860 the Liberian coastline had become 600 miles

Joseph Jenkins Roberts served as president of Liberia from 1848 to 1856 and again from 1872 to 1876.

(1,000 km) long. Meanwhile, Britain and France were gaining power in the region, and Liberia was no match for the European colonizers. Eventually, Liberia accepted payments and surrendered all land south of the Cavalla River to France and west of the Mano River to Britain.

Some local ethnic groups continued to fight. In 1855, Kru soldiers attacked Greenville harbor. Liberian troops defeated them and took over their land. In 1857, the Grebo people declared themselves independent and attacked Liberian settlers. The following year, the government agreed to grant the Grebo people full rights as citizens as long as they joined the republic. It was not until ninety years later that all sixteen Liberian ethnic groups were granted full citizenship.

The Kru people live in southern Liberia. Traditionally, they were known as seafarers.

Turbulent Times

The Americo-Liberians, as the emigrants from the United States and their descendants came to be called, controlled the government even though they were less than 5 percent of the population. Their political party, the True Whig Party, was in power from independence until 1980. In the early 1900s, the Whigs strengthened their control by creating districts in the interior and requiring local leaders to report to the central

Rubber workers carry buckets full of latex, a sticky liquid they drain from rubber trees.

government. To support the country's economy, the Whigs imposed oppressive laws and taxes. Despite the income from taxes, Liberia's economy was failing. The government turned to foreign powers to invest in the country. American and European companies were aware that Liberia had many desirable natural resources, such as iron, gold, and timber. However, the country's infrastructure—roads, railways, and bridges—was inadequate for transporting goods to market. A British mining company was the first to invest money by building roads in exchange for mining ore. Other mining and timber companies followed. In the United States, automobiles were becoming increasingly popular. Rubber was needed for tires, and Liberia's climate was ideally suited for growing rubber trees. In 1926, the American rubber company Firestone leased more than 1 million acres (400,000 hectares) near Monrovia. The company planted rubber trees, built roads and railways, and provided many new jobs for people. During World War II, rubber consumption increased and the U.S. Army built a deepwater port to load rubber onto large ships.

In 1944, William V. S. Tubman was elected president. During his twenty-seven years as the country's leader he encouraged development through a plan he called the Open Door Policy, which gave large tax benefits to foreign companies willing to trade with Liberia. While the economy improved, the environment suffered because of bad mining and logging practices. Although some indigenous Liberians had better job opportunities, it was mostly the Americo-Liberians who got rich. The divide between rich and poor grew wider. The poor had little access to good jobs, education, transportation, clean water, or electricity. Tubman died in 1971, and his vice president, William R. Tolbert Jr., inherited a failing economy and a society that was falling apart. Tolbert tried to make improvements. One of his ideas was to raise taxes on imported rice. People, especially the poor, relied on rice as the main staple of their diet. The president thought that higher prices on imported rice would encourage people to grow rice for their families and to sell at markets. The idea backfired. People protested angrily in what came to be called the Rice Riots.

Violence and Disorder

By the end of the 1970s, indigenous Liberians had grown outraged by government corruption and favoritism among politicians and wealthy Americo-Liberians. An ethnic Krahn army master sergeant named Samuel Kanyon Doe plotted to take over the government. On the night of April 12, 1980, he and a small group of soldiers entered the president's mansion and assassinated Tolbert. In the morning, Doe announced they had taken over the government. On April 22, after a trial in name only, thirteen leading members of Tolbert's government were executed by firing squad. At first, Liberians were shocked by the murders. But later, many saw hope that the new government might come to favor the majority of the people and not the wealthy few.

Doe and his group formed a political party called the People's Redemption Council (PRC). They focused on dismantling the old government and suspended the nation's constitution. The PRC imprisoned, tortured, and assassinated former government officials and wealthy Americo-Liberians. But Doe and his followers had no government or leadership experience, and were unable to make true reforms or construct a functional government. In 1985, elections were held amid threats, fraud, and corruption. Doe declared himself president, although many election observers said that he had actually lost to his opponent. He was Liberia's first indigenous leader. Doe became obsessed with protecting himself from outsiders. He appointed mostly friends and other ethnic Krahns to leadership positions. He shut down newspapers and outlawed public gatherings. He mistreated other ethnic groups. Eventually, the PRC's policies and practices led to widespread distrust and resentment among all Liberians.

Doe's rebellion did not last. The man behind PRC's end was named Charles Taylor. Taylor was a member of the wealthy

Americo-Liberian class. He had earned a degree in economics in the United States. Upon returning to Liberia, he became a high-ranking government official. In 1983, Doe accused Taylor of stealing money. Taylor fled to the United States. The United States imprisoned him on behalf of Liberia, and Doe asked the United States to return him to Liberia. However, Taylor escaped to Libya where he formed an army and founded a new political party called the National Patriotic Front of Liberia (NPFL).

In 1989, Taylor and his soldiers invaded Liberia. Many Americo-Liberians fled the country. But many indigenous Liberians supported him because they had turned against Doe. One of Taylor's men, Prince Johnson, broke away and formed his own army. Johnson led a group of soldiers who captured, tortured, and ultimately murdered President Doe.

From 1989 to 1996, one of the world's most violent civil wars raged in Liberia. The armies of Taylor, Johnson, and the Liberian government paralyzed the nation. Villages were

Samuel Kanyon Doe, shortly after taking over the government in April 1980

raided and burned, and people were kidnapped, tortured, and murdered. Children were captured, starved, drugged, and forced to become soldiers. More than 250,000 Liberians lost their lives in the fighting, and hundreds of thousands more fled to refugee camps in neighboring countries. In 1997, an election was held and Charles Taylor was selected to be president. Most say that people voted for him out of fear.

Under Charles Taylor's rule, Liberians lived with increasing poverty, unemployment, fear, and hopelessness. The country needed to recover from civil war. It needed rebuilding—new

Soldiers from the Krahn ethnic group battle Charles Taylor's forces during the first civil war.

roads and schools, clean water, and electricity. Instead, Taylor concerned himself with strengthening his army, gathering wealth and power, and taking over parts of Guinea and Sierra Leone. In 1999, rebel groups formed in these two countries to oppose Taylor, but they also opposed each other. These developments produced Liberia's second civil war. Going after Taylor, the rebels raided, plundered, tortured, and murdered villagers in brutal surprise attacks. The United States embassy in Monrovia was bombed, killing many civilians who had taken shelter there. Some U.S. troops arrived, as well as soldiers from other African countries. But violence continued and nations around the world called Taylor a ruthless warlord and ceased trading with Liberia, destroying the economy and further harming the livelihoods of the people.

United Nations peacekeeping forces patrol in Liberia in 2003, to help bring stability to the country.

Women in Monrovia protest in 2003, demanding peace.

An End to War

In 2003, a group of women formed an organization called the Women of Liberia Mass Action for Peace, led by a social worker named Leymah Gbowee. Their goal was to speak to Charles Taylor and demand an end to war. In the beginning, Gbowee went to her Christian church and enlisted several hundred women to join her to pray for peace. They held public prayer sessions. Soon, Muslim women joined them, and eventually three thousand women belonged to the organization. The women, followed by children, marched through the streets of Monrovia chanting and carrying banners saying "The women of Liberia want peace now." Thousands of women staged demonstrations at a fish market outside of the presidential mansion. Dressed in white clothing, the women prayed, danced, and sang for peace. Charles Taylor eventually met with them and agreed to attend peace talks. Three weeks later, Taylor resigned and went into exile. The women decided to work to help the

Mighty Be Her Powers

In 1989, Leymah Gbowee was just a teenager when the Liberian civil war erupted. She said she "turned from being a child into an adult in a matter of hours." Amid the years of fighting, she became a mother and a social worker, working with ex-child soldiers.

One night, Gbowee dreamt that peace could be possible if women would rally against the brutal conduct of soldiers, of whom nearly all were men. She organized the movement called Women of Liberia Mass Action for Peace, in which thousands of women from diverse ethnic backgrounds and religious faiths called out to the warlords to stop fighting. After the women convinced Charles Taylor to attend peace talks in Ghana, many chose to follow him, to enforce his participation. At one point, Taylor and his soldiers prepared to walk out of the talks and Gbowee and two hundred women joined hands and encircled the

doorways. Police arrived, threatened the women, and tried to arrest Gbowee. Gbowee responded by threatening to take off her clothes. Removing her clothes in public would be an enormous taboo, which according to traditional beliefs would curse and shame the men. The women's resistance became the turning point at the peace talks. A cease-fire was signed and three weeks later Charles Taylor resigned. Taylor ultimately was tried as a war criminal at The Hague in the Netherlands and sentenced to fifty years in prison.

Gbowee has continued her activism. She cofounded the Women Peace and Security Network for Africa as well as the Gbowee Peace Foundation Africa. Both organizations provide education and leadership training for women and girls. She has written a book about her experiences called *Mighty Be Our Powers*. In 2011, Gbowee was awarded the Nobel Peace Prize for her efforts to heal her country.

country hold new elections. For two years, they registered voters and set up polling places. In 2005, Liberia elected Ellen Johnson Sirleaf, the first woman in Africa to be elected president. In 2011, Johnson Sirleaf was reelected.

Recovery

As fourteen years of violent civil war came to an end, President Johnson Sirleaf and her Unity Party were burdened with enormous responsibility. An economist and an experienced leader, Johnson Sirleaf made certain that all people would be represented in the government, which includes a diversity of political parties and ethnic groups. She encouraged Liberians who had fled

In recent years, Liberia has undertaken a major effort to construct public buildings and extend roads throughout the country.

The Palava Hut

In 2013, President Ellen Johnson Sirleaf (right) announced that the National Human Rights Commission would run a countrywide Palava Hut program to bring peace and understanding to war-torn communities. The commission called on traditional leaders, chiefs, elders, political parties, religious groups, and citizens to gather together in village meeting places called palava huts and discuss the war and its aftermath. Traditionally, a palava hut is a round building where disputes are settled. It is located in a community's central courtyard. In the National Palava Hut Program, soldiers and victims are asked to tell their war-related stories. People who committed war crimes have the opportunity to admit their wrongdoing and ask for forgiveness. Villagers and their leaders together decide on what the atonement or punishment should be. The word *palava* comes from a mixture of French and English words used by early traders. It means "to communicate." The government sees the National Palava Hut Program as a "space where truth is sacred" and the best way to heal and unite communities broken by war.

the country to return and contribute to society. She urged foreign companies and governments to return and invest in Liberia.

The United Nations maintains a peacekeeping army in Liberia. The economy has improved, and goals have been set for rebuilding infrastructure, improving basic services, expanding education, and developing more jobs. The government's efforts are headed in the right direction, but there lies a long history of distrust and tension between ethnic groups. To that, the president said, "We cannot change our history; let us accept it for what it is and go forward."

CHAPTER 5

The Love of Liberty

THE PRESENT GOVERNMENT OF LIBERIA HAS EVOLVED slowly. Over the course of many centuries, people of sixteen ethnic groups migrated into what is now Liberia. The last migration occurred in the nineteenth century when Americo-Liberians arrived, some from the United States, others rescued from slave ships. Although the original groups shared many similarities in their political systems, they did not share a unified government. It was not until the arrival of the Americo-Liberians that a central government began to form.

The Central Government

When the Americo-Liberians settled in Monrovia and established a government, they chose the motto, "The Love of Liberty Brought Us Here." Many of the original settlers who

The Lone Star Flag

The flag of Liberia has symbols also found in the American flag. In the upper left corner is a single white star on a blue square. The white star represents the freedom of the formerly enslaved Africans and Americans who came to Liberia. The color blue represents liberty and justice, and the blue square represents the African mainland. Eleven equal stripes alternating red and white run across the flag. Eleven is the number of people who signed Liberia's declaration of independence. Red represents bravery and dignity, and white represents purity. The flag was adopted in 1847.

arrived in 1822 or soon after were freeborn black Americans who were generally well educated. In the first years of the settlement, white ACS agents governed. In 1847, however, the settlers declared their independence and became the first democratic republic in Africa to be governed by black people. Americo-Liberians became the governing class.

Around the time of independence, five counties plus the city of Monrovia had been accepted into the republic. All the counties were situated along the coast within relatively easy access to Monrovia, the capital. The rest of the country was divided into three provinces: Eastern, Central, and Western. By the mid-twentieth century, indigenous people were protesting their lack of representation, and the Liberian government began creating new counties. Today, Liberia is divided into fifteen counties and the capital city of Monrovia. Monrovia, like Washington, D.C., is governed directly by the federal government and has no senators or representatives in the National Assembly.

A Look at Monrovia

Monrovia, the capital of Liberia, is by far the largest city in the country and the leading business and commercial center. Home to more than one million people, the city sprawls across many neighborhoods. Yet Monrovia also has fine boulevards, historic buildings, galleries, parks, shops, hotels, restaurants, and a bustling waterfront market. Limousines and taxis transport the wealthy to their stately houses and lush gardens. Office and government workers, technology and construction workers, shopkeepers, and other middle class people enjoy a comfortable lifestyle. But Monrovia also has dirt and potholed roads where men push wheelbarrows loaded with tools or goods for market and women carry baskets and bundles gracefully on their heads.

Monrovia is leading the country in its recovery from war. The city suffered more losses than most, as the various factions fought many battles in the capital. The National Museum of Liberia, once home to more than five thousand paintings, sculptures, and artifacts, was looted of nearly its entire collection during the second civil war. Today, museum workers are rebuilding and adding contemporary African art as well as ancient local art to its collection.

Just north of the center of the capital city of Monrovia is tiny Providence Island, the landing site and first settlement of the emigrants from America. Other islands surround the city and to the east is the large industrial area of the Freeport of Monrovia.

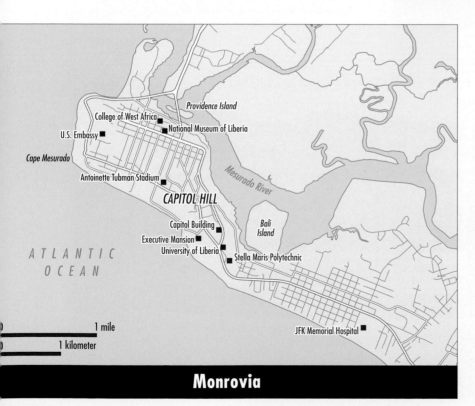

Monrovia

College of West Africa
Providence Island
National Museum of Liberia
U.S. Embassy
Cape Mesurado
Mesurado River
Antoinette Tubman Stadium
CAPITOL HILL
Bali Island
Capitol Building
Executive Mansion
University of Liberia
Stella Maris Polytechnic
ATLANTIC OCEAN
1 mile
1 kilometer
JFK Memorial Hospital

The Constitution

Liberia's first constitution was adopted in 1847. Modeled on the U.S. Constitution, it created a federal government with three branches: executive, legislative, and judicial. The constitution granted freedom of speech, freedom of religion, the right to assemble, and the right to pursue the enjoyment of life and liberty, and to own and defend personal property. The constitution also declared that only "persons of color" could be granted citizenship, that slavery was prohibited, that women were allowed to own or inherit property, and that indigenous people were

The Executive Mansion in Monrovia serves as both the home and the offices of the president.

Liberia's National Government

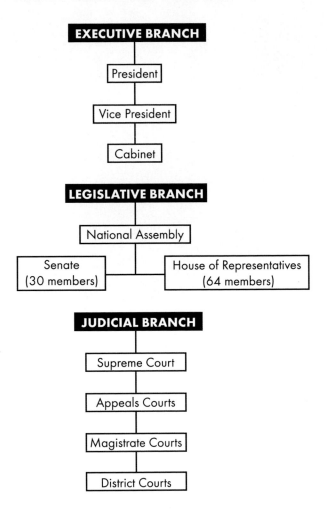

EXECUTIVE BRANCH

President

Vice President

Cabinet

LEGISLATIVE BRANCH

National Assembly

Senate (30 members)

House of Representatives (64 members)

JUDICIAL BRANCH

Supreme Court

Appeals Courts

Magistrate Courts

District Courts

not allowed to own property. Because only male citizens who owned property were eligible to vote, the vote was denied to women and indigenous Liberians. This changed in 1946, when indigenous people and women were granted the right to vote.

The Liberian constitution was suspended in 1980 when Samuel Doe took over the government. A new constitution

In 2013, Axel Addy became the minister of commerce and industry. This ministry focuses on expanding agriculture, tourism, and other businesses.

was adopted in 1986, and it remains the law of the land today. The current constitution states that everyone has the right to employment regardless of sex, religion, ethnic background, birthplace, or political affiliation, and that all people are entitled to equal pay for equal work.

Executive Branch

The president of Liberia is the head of state, the head of government, and the commander in chief of the armed forces. The president is elected to a six-year term and may be reelected for one additional term. The president along with the vice president and the cabinet ministers form the executive branch of the government. The president appoints the cabinet ministers with the approval of the Senate. There are nineteen cabinet

A Female First

Ellen Johnson was born in 1938, in Monrovia, Liberia. Although she was raised in Americo-Liberian society, her grandmothers were indigenous villagers who could not read or write. Johnson was fortunate to be able to attend school. She studied accounting at the College of West Africa and at age seventeen married her husband, James Sirleaf. She attended Harvard University in the United States and then returned to Liberia and worked in President Tolbert's government. When Samuel Doe assassinated President Tolbert, Johnson Sirleaf fled the country. After working as a banker in Kenya, she returned to Liberia and ran for Senate. During the campaign, however, she was arrested

and sentenced to ten years in prison for speaking out against Doe's military regime. She was released after serving part of her sentence and again left the country.

In 1997, she returned to Liberia and ran for office against Charles Taylor. After Taylor won, he accused Johnson Sirleaf of treason, and once again she was forced to flee. She did not return to Liberia until Taylor resigned. In 2005, she ran for president and won, becoming Africa's first elected female head of state. She immediately pursued a course of economic recovery, encouraging foreign investors to establish businesses in Liberia. She fought to rid the government of favoritism and corruption, and took up the cause of education reform and women's rights. Johnson Sirleaf was reelected president in 2011.

ministers who oversee government departments such as agriculture, labor, finance, defense, and commerce.

The president also has the power to appoint judges, ambassadors to foreign countries, local officials, and military officers, all of whom must also be approved by the Senate. An important duty of the president is to sign into law bills passed by the legislature, or to veto them. If there is a presidential veto, the legislature may vote to override the veto, but they must have a two-thirds majority to do so. The president may declare a state of emergency and suspend civil liberties (such as the

Members of the National Assembly listen to a speech by President Ellen Johnson Sirleaf.

right to assemble) in the event of war, violent demonstrations, or catastrophes. The state of emergency must be approved by a two-thirds majority of the National Assembly within seven days, or the order must be lifted.

Legislative Branch

Liberia's legislature, called the National Assembly, is divided into two chambers, the Senate and the House of Representatives. There are thirty senators. Each of the fifteen counties elects two senators to nine-year terms. The House of Representatives has sixty-four members. Each is elected from a district that includes approximately an equal number of voters. Members of the House of Representatives are elected to six-year terms.

Judicial Branch

The highest court in the judicial system is the Supreme Court. The president appoints the chief justice and four associate justices. Below the Supreme Court are appeals courts, magistrate courts, and district courts.

Many towns and villages also have local traditional courts. In many cases, smaller crimes such as petty thefts, disputes between villagers, divorce settlements, or public misbehavior are handled by traditional chiefs. In Muslim communities, citizens may also seek out justice in an imam's court. Instead of handing down punishments, local court judges often tell the accused to seek forgiveness and make amends to the community.

Village Governments

Villagers today continue to follow some form of their traditional government systems. The Kissi people live in small villages with a public square that includes the home of the village headman. The Kissi honor their elders. The head elder leads ceremonies and acts as a judge within the community. The Kpelle, the largest ethnic group, is organized into many chiefdoms, or towns. Each chiefdom is divided into districts, and each district has a leader or commissioner that represents his people to the paramount, or leading, chief. The paramount chiefs officially interact between their chiefdoms and the central Liberian government. Paramount chiefs also maintain their traditional roles of settling disputes, keeping the peace, and maintaining village infrastructure.

The Gio people divide their villages into quarters. Each quarter is made up of an extended family. The quarters are led by a quarter chief who is usually the oldest male in the family. A council of elders, however, holds greater authority. The headman of a Krahn village is generally the most skilled. He is usually the most successful farmer, hunter, and fisher. The leader is assisted by a council consisting of successful young men and elders. The leader and the council act as judges

National Anthem

Daniel Bashiel Warner, the third president of Liberia, wrote the words to "All Hail, Liberia, Hail!" the country's national anthem. The music is by Olmstead Luca. It was adopted as the national anthem in 1847.

All hail, Liberia, hail!
All hail, Liberia, hail!
This glorious land of liberty,
Shall long be ours.
Though new her name,
Great be her fame,
And mighty be her powers,
And mighty be her powers.
In joy and gladness,
With our hearts united,
We'll shout the freedom,
Of a race benighted.
Long live Liberia, happy land!
A home of glorious liberty,
By God's command!
A home of glorious liberty,
By God's command!

and also oversee trade with other groups. The Kru are more democratic than many of the other groups in that the village chief is more of a representative than a figure of authority. Villagers elect their leader based on the person's character and diplomatic skills and not because of family background or age. Formerly, traditional governments developed their government around clans and ruling families, but today more village leaders are elected.

CHAPTER 6

Rain Forest Riches

FOR CENTURIES, FARMING, HUNTING, AND CRAFTING tools, pots, baskets, and other useful items sustained the nation's people. But following the arrival of the Americo-Liberians, changes occurred. Coffee, rubber, and shipping grew as important industries. However, natural resources, traditional skills, and small-scale commerce still make up a good portion of the nation's economic activities. Though Liberia is one of the poorest countries in the world, it has the potential and resources to progress and build its wealth.

Working the Land

The Liberian economy is based on agriculture. Liberians grow an enormous variety of food. The abundance is seen everywhere, in supermarkets, at local outdoor markets, and on loading docks waiting to be shipped to other countries. Among the many crops especially enjoyed by Liberians are sweet potatoes, rice, cassava, plantains, peanuts, corn, bananas, and melons. In small family gardens, people grow beans, tomatoes, onions, and peppers. Foods grown for export include sugarcane, cocoa, coffee, and palm oil.

Rice is the most important food for rural Liberian families. Families and villages work together to grow rice. Many farmers grow rice with the traditional slash and burn method. In the dry season, farmers, usually the men, clear a section of forest with simple hand tools and burn the brush. They leave behind large stumps to keep the soil from washing away. Later, women and children play important roles, hoeing, planting, and weeding.

Liberian women harvest rice, the main source of food for many Liberian people.

They also harvest the crop, which is a time to celebrate. The rice grows during the rainy season. Rice farmers produce only one crop each year. Once the rice is harvested, the soil has been drained of its nutrients, and the field is abandoned. The next year, a new field is cut. After seven years, the soil renews itself and farmers can return to a field and grow another crop of rice.

Many farmers also raise livestock, mostly cattle and goats. Some families raise chickens, but businesspeople are developing new commercial poultry farms. People also fish and hunt wild game.

Liberia's climate and soil are ideal for growing tree crops such as

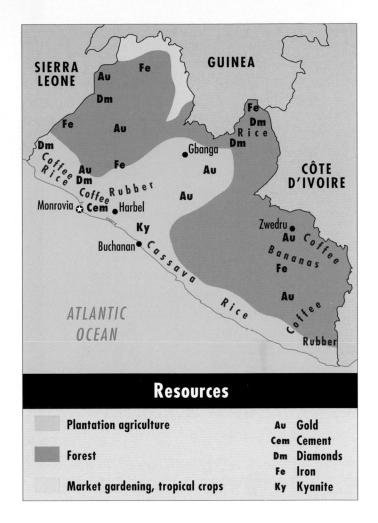

cocoa, palm oil, coconuts, and rubber. These crops are grown on large plantations. Rubber plantations are the largest non-government employer in the country. Although most rubber plantations are owned by foreign corporations, 30 percent of the rubber trees are grown on small independent farms. The independent rubber growers tend their own trees on their own land and sell their rubber to the major plantations. Rubber is Liberia's main export, and the country is the sixth-largest producer of rubber in the world.

Firestone

In 1926, Harvey Firestone offered just six cents an acre to the government of Liberia to lease one million acres of land for ninety-nine years. He then created the largest rubber tree plantation in the world. Although the deal had a clear advantage for Firestone, Liberia also benefited. The company built railroads, roads, and bridges, as well as employee housing, health clinics, and schools, basically importing an American lifestyle. The new roads and railways linked Guinea, Monrovia, and Côte d'Ivoire.

When Liberia's first civil war broke out, the rubber tree plantations were looted by the warlords and many were left to deteriorate. The Firestone company continued to operate, but profits fell drastically as Charles Taylor and his forces took over the area. After the war, Firestone began the task of replanting and rebuilding roads, schools, employees' homes, and farm buildings. In order to help the independent growers restart their businesses, the company gave them six hundred thousand rubber tree saplings to plant.

Natural Resources

Liberia is rich in natural resources, with abundant timber and deep deposits of iron ore, diamonds, and gold. Iron-ore mining is a major industrial activity, and iron is the nation's second-largest export product. In the years before the first civil war, Liberia was Africa's leading iron exporter and one of the largest iron exporters in the world. The war damaged mines and destroyed railways and roads, as well as the shipping port of Buchanan. International mining companies are beginning to reinvest in rebuilding mines and infrastructure.

What Liberia Grows, Makes, and Mines

AGRICULTURE (2011)

Cassava	495,000 metric tons
Rice	300,000 metric tons
Rubber	63,000 metric tons

MANUFACTURING (2013)

Cement	200,000 metric tons

MINING (2011)

Iron	1,300,000 metric tons
Diamonds	41,932 carats
Gold	469 kilograms

Rain forest hardwoods are a valuable resource. Forty percent of Liberia is covered in forest. In the past, logging was done without much concern for the environment. International logging companies cut down wide swaths of forests. During the war, Charles Taylor controlled nearly 85 percent of all logging. The money from timber supplied his armies with weapons and other goods. In an effort to reduce Taylor's power, the United Nations imposed a ban on all timber sales coming from Liberian forests. The ban was lifted in 2006. The government still battles illegal logging, but it is making progress. The United States, European Union, and responsible logging companies are working with Liberia to better manage the forests. An important part of their plan is to use 30 percent of the income from logging to improve the

lives of the people who live in the rain forests. Investors and the government are also working with local companies to develop new businesses, such as portable sawmills, plywood processing plants, and kilns for drying lumber. Instead of shipping raw timber overseas, these businesses would provide new jobs and additional income for the country.

Besides iron ore, Liberia also mines gold and diamonds. Most of the diamonds are mined by small companies. In 2001, during the war, Liberia exported more than 150,000 carats of diamonds per year. Once again, Charles Taylor took over a valuable resource. He used diamond mining to fund his rebel regime. The United Nations acted by banning the export of Liberian diamonds. Diamonds sold to fund wars are called conflict diamonds, or "blood diamonds." After Taylor left the country, the new government appealed to the United Nations to lift the ban on conflict diamonds. It was lifted in 2007. Slowly, Liberia has started to rebuild its diamond mining industry. Four years after the ban, Liberia mined 42,000 carats of diamonds. Although this is far below the amount before the ban, production is on the rise and investors are searching for new diamond deposits.

Manufacturing

Little manufacturing happens in Liberia. While there are many craftspeople skilled in traditional arts, such as pottery, basket weaving, woodworking, or metalworking, most people buy and use inexpensive imported products from countries such as India or China. Aid organizations are working in cities and towns trying to help people establish small factories to manufacture such items as clothing, plywood, and computer parts. In 2013, the Ministry of Commerce began developing plants to process cassava, a staple of the Liberian diet that can be turned into many different products. It is the government's goal to see manufacturing become a greater part of the economy.

Energy

The lack of available and affordable energy is Liberia's largest obstacle to development. Electricity is not widely available in villages, towns, or cities, including Monrovia. In 1960, the Mount Coffee Dam, a large hydroelectric power plant on the St. Paul River, began generating power and supplying electricity to Monrovia and nearby cities. During the war, Charles Taylor's soldiers raided the plant and ordered workers to leave. Heavy rains were falling and the water behind the dam was building up. Without experienced workers who knew how to open the dam's gates to release water pressure, the dam blew up. Monrovia was left in darkness. The Mount Coffee Dam has been undergoing repair for many years. New turbines are now ready to generate efficient and affordable electricity and workers are stringing power lines to cities. There are small hydropower stations throughout the country that produce a little electricity for some towns. Still, more than two-thirds of the country relies on wood and charcoal for energy. People use batteries or expensive gas-fueled generators to run their homes and businesses.

Money Facts

The Liberian dollar is Liberia's official currency, abbreviated L$. However, U.S. currency also circulates. Paper bills come in values of 5, 10, 20, 50, and 100 Liberian dollars and coins come in values of 1, 5, 10, 25, and 50 cents. There is also a 1-dollar coin.

Each paper bill shows an image of a Liberian president, such as Samuel Doe, who is on the 50-dollar bill. On the 10-dollar bill is the likeness of Joseph Jenkins Roberts, Liberia's first president. As a nickname, the bill is often called a "J.J."

On the back of the 10-dollar bill is an image of a man removing rubber from a rubber tree and the seal of the Central Bank of Liberia. The seal shows two crossed iron rods. The iron rod was a traditional form of currency called a Kissi penny. Above the crossed Kissi pennies is the front of a 50-cent coin depicting the profile of Lady Liberty, surrounded by the words *Republic of Liberia*. Below the profile is a single star. Under the crossed Kissi pennies is an image of the back of the coin, which carries the date and a circle of olive branches. In 2015, L$92 equaled US$1.

Transportation

Transportation needs in Liberia are great. Major infrastructure such as paved roads and railways are extremely lacking. Most roads are dirt. Rain floods roads and creates enormous potholes and huge mountains of red mud, all making travel inland often impossible. Liberia has 66,000 miles (106,000 km) of roads and only 7 percent are paved. Foreign governments and aid organizations are helping to improve roads and repair railroad tracks damaged by war. With better roads, more children will be able to take a bus to school and people will have easier access to hospitals and markets. Farmers and growers will be able to get their fruits and vegetables to market before they spoil. Large companies involved in mining, logging, and agriculture are assisting in road building and repairing and expanding railways to get their products to market. Very few Liberians own a car or truck. Although Monrovia's streets are jammed with taxis, cars, buses, and trucks, most people throughout the country walk or take minibuses.

A rough red road leads through the wilderness in eastern Liberia. Gradually, roads throughout Liberia are being paved.

Cranes lift giant containers at the Port of Monrovia.

Travel by water is Liberia's most efficient form of transportation. There are few overland routes to deliver exports and imports to and from markets, so nearly all of the country's exports and imports pass through Monrovia or other ports such as Buchanan or Greenville. The Freeport of Monrovia is one of the busiest in the world. A freeport is a type of harbor where ships can unload cargo, store cargo, and load cargo onto other ships without paying government duties or taxes.

Communications

After years of civil war, broadcasters and publishers worked hard to restore their services. There are six major English language newspapers and one state-run radio station in Liberia. Numerous other radio stations are operated by international organizations, such as the United Nations and ELWA Radio, Africa's first Christian radio station. Liberia has a satellite station. A fair por-

Oceangoing tankers, containerships, and cruise liners all must fly a country's flag from their decks. Prior to the twentieth century, ships flew the flag of the shipowner's country, which required the ship to follow all the country's laws, even when sailing in another part of the world. After World War II, America's secretary of state made a stop in Monrovia and saw how poor the country was. He suggested that Liberia earn income by offering a "flag of convenience." A flag of convenience program allows shipowners to register their ships with any country, fly its flag, and operate under that country's laws.

Liberia charges less to register a ship than other countries and its labor laws for employees are less strict. This makes the Liberia registry very popular. For example, the ship at the left is owned by a German but registered in Liberia. Liberia has the second-largest ships' registry in the world, after Panama. More than 3,600 ships carry more than 100 million tons of cargo each year while flying the Liberian flag. In fact, 11 percent of ships worldwide, including 35 percent of the world's tanker fleet, fly the Liberian flag. Liberia's flag of convenience registry is an important and steady source of income and was the only source of income that did not suffer during the civil wars.

tion of the population has access to the Internet through cell phones. Throughout the country, vendors operate small cell phone charging stalls and sell pay-as-you-go cell phone minutes. Low-cost cell phones and social media give Liberians access to news, economic and political developments, and each other like never before. In 2014, when the country faced a deadly outbreak of the Ebola virus, health authorities used texts and social media to spread the word about the disease, its symptoms, its treatments, the location of health clinics, and disease prevention measures.

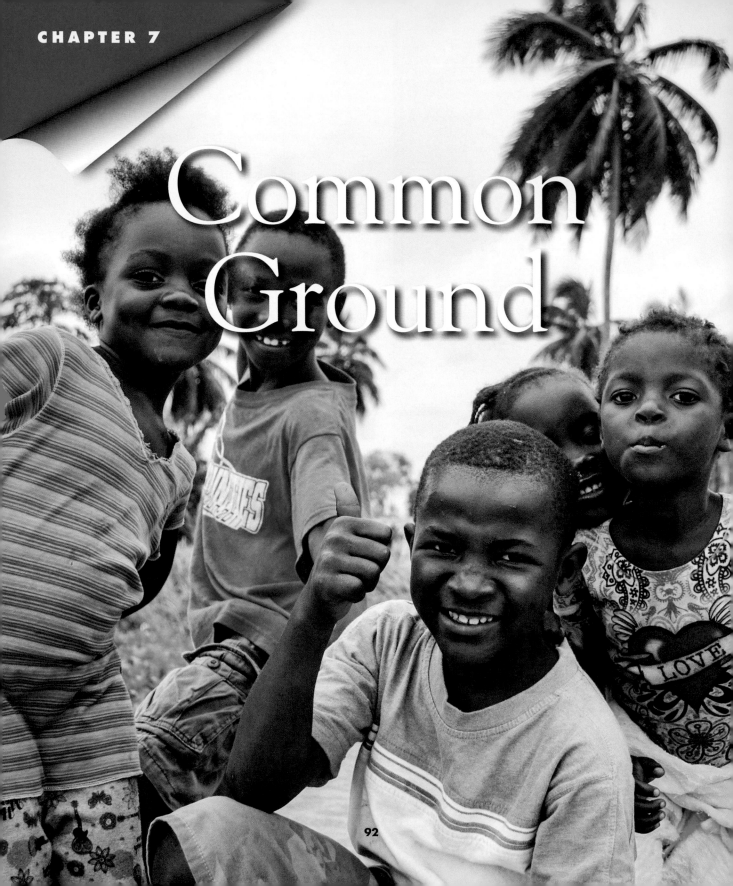

CHAPTER 7

Common Ground

THE REPUBLIC OF LIBERIA WAS BORN IN THE NINETEENTH century, when the colonists came from the United States and settled along the Atlantic coast. They lived on land that had traditionally been the home to sixteen different ethnic groups. Within a few decades, people who identified socially and culturally with a group suddenly became countrymen and countrywomen. Relationships were often tense. The indigenous peoples resented the newcomers for controlling the central government and the colonizers were wary of the unfamiliar ways of the indigenous groups. Furthermore, there were long-standing feuds between some of the sixteen ethnic groups. But as time passed, Liberians faced many challenges together, including civil war, poverty, and disease. Now, many of the different groups live and work side by side in the cities, and people from different groups have married. New bonds among people are forming and growing stronger.

Opposite: **More than 43 percent of the people in Liberia are under age fifteen. By comparison, only 20 percent of Americans are younger than fifteen.**

A woman from the Kpelle group weaves a bag from a palm fiber. The Kpelle people live primarily in central Liberia.

Ethnic Groups

The groups that migrated to Liberia came in waves. The larger groups later divided into smaller groups and clans. There are three main linguistic groups, meaning groups of people who share a common, or related, language. Some of the first people to arrive were Mel speakers. This group has since separated into the Gola and Kissi peoples. The Bandi, Gio, Kpelle, Loma, Mandingo, Mano, Mende, and Vai groups are all Mande speakers. They began arriving in the fifteenth century from the northern grasslands of Guinea and Sudan. The third language group is the Kru. Kru-speaking groups are the Bassa, Bella, Dei, Grebo, Krahn, and Kru. Besides English, there are dozens of different dialects, or regional languages.

Mande language speakers generally live in the northwest and central areas of Liberia, Kru speakers reside in the south, and Mel language speakers live along the northern border and northwest coast. The Kpelle, in the central part of Liberia, is the largest group, making up 20 percent of the population. The second-largest group is the Bassa, who make up 14 percent. The Gio, Mano, and Kru make up the rest of the top-five most populous groups. The most common languages spoken in the capital city of Monrovia are English, Bassa, and Kru.

Immigrant Populations

There is a small minority of people from outside Africa who call Liberia home. The largest group is from Lebanon, a region in the Middle East, where Asia and Africa meet. In the middle of the

Ethnicity in Liberia (2008 est.)	
Kpelle	20.1%
Bassa	13.4%
Grebo	10.0%
Gio	8.0%
Mano	7.9%
Kru	6.0%
Loma	5.1%
Kissi	4.8%
Gola	4.4%
Others, including Americo-Liberians	20.1%

The Talking Drum

A talking drum is a traditional West African instrument. It is an hourglass-shaped drum that can mimic the rhythm and tone of human speech. Storytellers and local historians used the drums to preserve their culture and help them remember important people or events. The talking drums were also used as a form of communication. Local leaders sent drummers to other villages to alert them to good or bad news. Villagers may not have understood the foreign language, but they understood the language of the drum and responded accordingly. Talking drums continue to be used in celebrations and rituals and for reconciling disputes between people. Although cell phones, television, and radios have taken over many of the roles the talking drum once played, the drum remains part of a grand heritage and still speaks to the people.

nineteenth century, when Lebanon was facing economic trouble, Lebanese Christians and later Lebanese Muslims immigrated to Liberia. Many became successful businesspeople, owning supermarkets, movie theaters, restaurants, retail stores, hotels, and real estate. In the years since the civil wars, some Pakistani, Indian, and Chinese merchants have also moved to Liberia.

Liberian English

English is Liberia's official language. It is used in government, business, and in schools. Many people are bilingual, meaning they speak two languages. Slightly more than 20 percent of Liberians are English speakers, most of them city dwellers and government workers, although the numbers are growing among all groups of

A Liberian man speaks to a Chinese woman in Monrovia.

people. A simple form of English was spoken in Liberia before the colonists came, because English, mixed with some French and Portuguese, was the language used by European traders.

During the civil wars, many Liberians abandoned their homes and sought refuge in other areas or in other countries. English was the language they used to communicate with strangers. Today, English is becoming more widespread in rural villages due to improvements in education and the increase in cell phone and Internet use.

Traditional African languages sound musical. The tone is rhythmic and lilting. In everyday life, many people speak a form of English called Liberian English, which is a mixture of English slang, Standard English, and African languages. Liberian English, which is different in many ways from Standard English, has several versions. Standard Liberian English comes from African American spoken English. Other

A Way with Words

Here are some unique words and phrases that Liberians use to express themselves:

Word or Phrase	Meaning
Carry	To go with. "I will carry you home."
Cold water	To soothe bad feelings. "Here is cold water, I am sorry."
Dress	To move out of the way. "Dress small, my man." (Meaning "Please excuse me, sir." Adding "small" is to be polite).
Hang head	To meet, confer. "The men are hanging head at the club."
In the house	Privately. "The argument was settled in the house."
Reaching	To leave. "Good night. I reaching."
Small-Small	Little by little. "We are getting the job done small-small." also, No matter. "No worries, small-small."
Too-fine	Excellent. "Those shoes are too-fine."

versions are more like African English. There are hundreds of unique expressions, pronunciations, and proverbs, as well as differences in vocabulary. A common practice is to place an *o* at the end of a friendly or pleasant exchange, such as "Hello-o. How are you-o?" or "Thanks plenty-o!"

City and Country

Liberia has approximately four million citizens. A little less than half of the people live in cities or towns. About one-third of Liberians live in or near Monrovia, and more than 300,000 live in the large inland city of Gbanga. While there are Liberians who enjoy modern conveniences and have access to electricity, clean running water, good sanitation, schools, and dependable transportation, the vast majority of the population does not. Most city dwellers live in crowded housing without electricity and running water. Rural villagers fare even worse. They have virtually no access to decent roads, running water, electricity, and proper sanitation. Often, remote villages are at least an hour's walk from one another and several hours away from health clinics and schools. For the most part, villagers must rely on one another for food and support.

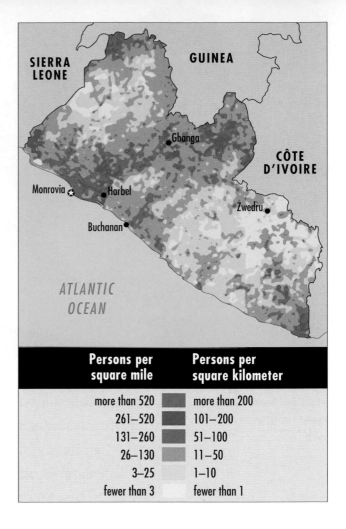

Education

Liberia is still developing its education system. Not every child has an opportunity to attend school, and many public and government schools are poorly run and poorly funded. It was not until 2007 that Liberia began free public education for all elementary school children. Prior to 2007, only people who could afford to pay for clothing, books, and supplies could attend school. Since free elementary education was introduced, the number of children in schools has increased dramatically, even though rural children must overcome many obstacles to attend. Some students attend schools run by aid organizations, missionaries, and churches. Those schools are usually more organized and better funded. But the government is making a big effort to improve the public education system. For example, the government worked with foreign aid organizations to build a

Persons per square mile		Persons per square kilometer
more than 520		more than 200
261–520		101–200
131–260		51–100
26–130		11–50
3–25		1–10
fewer than 3		fewer than 1

Population of Major Cities (2008 est.)

Monrovia	1,021,762
Gbanga	333,481
Buchanan	50,245
Zwedru	25,349
Harbel	25,309

Most students in Liberia wear uniforms.

model public school campus in Lofa County, in the northeast, that features solar panels to provide electricity for computers and a healthy free lunch for all students.

Beginning at age six, children may attend free elementary school. They study basic reading, English, arithmetic, and general science. After elementary school ends in sixth grade, students must pay school fees. Junior high school includes grades seven through nine. Students learn algebra, geometry, geography, physical science, and chemistry. When they have finished ninth grade, they must pass the West African Examinations Council test to receive a certificate. Students who pass can go to senior high school. Nearly all senior high schools are in Monrovia, and often only the children of well-to-do families attend.

Beyond senior high school, some graduates enroll in community colleges or vocational schools. Liberia has two state-run universities, the University of Liberia and the

Girls' Education

According to recent research, more than 40 percent of Liberian girls ages ten to fourteen have never gone to school. In many families, girls are expected to stay home and help with housework and care for younger children until they marry and move to their husband's home. Only 12 percent of girls attend high school and less than 20 percent of the students at the University of Liberia are female.

William V. S. Tubman University. There are also five private colleges run by Catholic, Episcopal, and Methodist churches. Many college-bound Liberians attend school in other countries, such as England and the United States.

When School Closed

In July 2014, schools closed in Liberia because of an Ebola virus outbreak. The deadly virus is extremely contagious, and health authorities warned people to avoid gathering in groups. When some concerned people learned that students were forced to stay home, they developed programs to help students continue to learn outside the classroom. Some children were given solar-powered or crank-powered laptops and tablets. For those who did not have access to the Internet, the tablets came preloaded with lessons. Another software company provided learning programs that could be downloaded onto cell phones. The Liberian government is determined to open up education opportunities for its young people and many around the world want to help achieve that goal.

CHAPTER 8

A Spiritual People

THE FIRST AMERICO-LIBERIANS WERE CHRISTIANS who named their settlement Christopolis, meaning "city of Christ." The Americo-Liberians were encouraged by their American sponsors to teach Christianity to the indigenous people. Although most people in Liberia are Christian, Liberia is not officially a Christian nation. The Liberian constitution grants people freedom of religion. High-ranking government officials take an oath of office on either a Christian Bible or the Muslim Qur'an. The government officially observes three religious holidays, Fast and Prayer Day, Thanksgiving, and Christmas. Regardless of faith, most Liberians attend a house of worship on those days.

Opposite: **Liberians pray at a Protestant church in Dolo Town, near Monrovia. Protestants are the largest religious group in Liberia.**

Early Beliefs

Many of the earliest people in West Africa held a belief in spirits called jinn. The name is related to the more familiar

Fast and Prayer Day

Fast and Prayer Day is a holiday that began during a political crisis between Liberia, Sierra Leone, and the British in the 1800s. Liberian leaders believed the only way to achieve peace was through fasting and praying. Ever since, the holiday has been celebrated as a day to pray for personal strength, healing, and the survival of the nation.

On Fast and Prayer Day, the second Friday in April, businesses are closed, and people attend church, avoid their daily activities, and fast. At 8 o'clock in the evening some people observe a Christian ritual called Sackcloth and Ashes. This ritual is an ancient form of protest for peace. Until noon the next day, people wear coarse garments made of sacks and sit on a bed of ashes, symbolizing humility and remorse. All through the night, they pray and meditate.

Arabic term *genie*. People believed that jinn were evil spirits that could take the shape of an animal or a person. The power of the spirit could be found in every living and nonliving thing, from trees to air to fire. Many people believed jinn could possess humans and trick them into committing sins. Only by magic could they be warded off.

Traditional Religions

Traditional West African religions share similar beliefs and practices. Many Liberian people, such as the Mende and the Gio, believe in a supreme being who created the universe and lives in heaven. The god is the source of both good and evil on Earth but does not interfere in the daily affairs of humans. There are also other lesser spirits, such as forest spirits and the spirits of dead people and animals. The Mende and others communicate to god or the spirits by praying to their ancestors who speak to god or the spirits for them. Family ties are powerful in indigenous societies and people respect their ancestors, whom they see as a link to one another and to the spirit world.

The Gio do not pray to the god, but rather to a spirit called Du, which is a spiritual power that connects people to god. The Du is believed to be the spirit within each person.

All Liberian ethnic groups have religious leaders who lead villagers in elaborate rites and rituals. During a ritual, the leader traditionally wears an intricate hand-carved wooden mask to disguise his human form. He, or rarely she, appears to become briefly possessed by spirits that help foresee the future, interpret omens, or seek blessings for the group. Many rituals

A Liberian religious leader performs a traditional ceremony for someone who has died.

include drumming, clapping, dancing, and chanting. Some practices include ritual healing of wounds or illnesses. These rites are lead by the healers, who are other important leaders. The healers prepare charms made of plants, shells, carvings, metal, and other objects. The charms protect against harmful spirits or cleanse a person who has broken a taboo (forbidden activity) or sinned against another person. Like the religious leaders, the healers also wear masks to disguise their human form and enter into a spiritual state of being.

The Kpelle believe in a supreme being who created the world and then departed. The being left behind blessings that give good health, good luck, and success to families. Traditional Vai religion believes in numerous spirits and in one god who is both good and evil.

Secret Societies

The most powerful religious practice among indigenous people is belonging to traditional secret societies. The practice in many of its forms is controversial but it continues to be a life-changing tradition. The secret societies, called Poro for boys and Sande for girls, are a rite of passage for teenagers. The boys and girls are taken out of school and the community and brought to forest sites where they are trained for several weeks in local lore, skills, and traditions. Girls are taught etiquette, good moral behavior, domestic skills, and child rearing, while boys are taught farming and hunting. But they are also forced to endure powerful, painful, and sometimes life-threatening rituals. The boys and girls are sworn to secrecy. Many of the

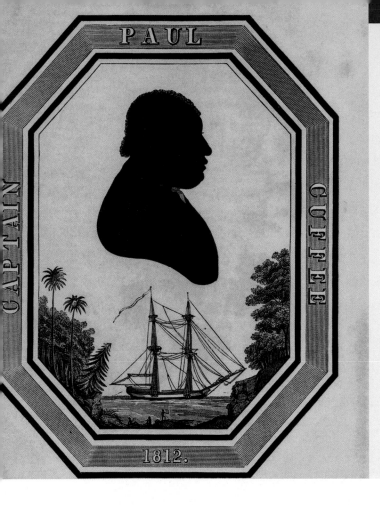

PAUL CUFFEE
CAPTAIN
1812.

A Quaker's Challenge

Paul Cuffee was a freeborn black American born in 1759 in Massachusetts. As a young man he worked on whaling ships and became a respected navigator. He began building his own ships and became one of the richest African Americans in the United States. Cuffee was a devout Quaker who was tormented by the existence of slavery. He envisioned a return of African Americans to Africa, where he believed there was opportunity to live in dignity and develop a prosperous settlement free from discrimination. He also longed to spread his Quaker beliefs to native Africans. Using his great wealth, he built and outfitted a ship and took a group of free black Americans to the coast of West Africa. They settled in Freetown in Sierra Leone. On his return to the United States, Cuffee made preparations for more voyages. He died before returning to Africa, but his efforts inspired the American Colonization Society and set in motion the colonizing of Liberia.

girls never return to school after Sande. Many Liberians and international women's groups are fighting to do away with the practice, including Ellen Johnson Sirleaf, who herself took part in a Sande ritual.

Christianity

The first Christian missionaries to Liberia were Methodists who arrived in the 1830s and 1840s. In the United States, their church had several outspoken ministers who called for the abolition of slavery. The Methodist Church became the largest Christian denomination in Liberia. Other Christian

Protestants followed, including Lutherans, Pentecostals, Seventh-Day Adventists, Baptists, Quakers, Zions, Mormons, and Episcopalians. Roman Catholics came to Liberia in 1906.

Christian missionaries answered many material needs of the people. Christian groups started most grade schools, vocational schools, and universities. Lutherans established the College of West Africa, Episcopalians the Cuttington University, Baptists the Lott Carey Mission School and Ricks Institute, and Roman Catholics the Stella Maris Polytechnic.

Mandingo women sing during a traditional naming ceremony following the birth of a child. Many Liberians practice both Christianity and traditional religions.

Christian groups run orphanages, grade schools, junior high and high schools, hospitals, and food, housing, and farming assistance programs for the poor. The missions gave the Liberian government a model to follow for developing its public schools, health care system, and social services.

When Christian missionaries first came to Liberia, many established themselves in Monrovia or along the coast. But eventually they moved inland to reach the remote villages. Traditional religions controlled all aspects of society, culture, and everyday life. The missionaries offered people education and assistance in daily living, and eventually most groups accepted the teachings of Christianity. Today, in rural villages especially, many Liberians practice a blend of Christianity and traditional religions.

Islam and Other Faiths

Between 12 and 20 percent of Liberians are Muslim. The Vai and Mandingo groups arrived in Liberia as practicing Muslims. Over time, other groups such as the Mende, Gola, and Gbandi slowly adopted Islamic beliefs while holding on to their indigenous traditions. There are six mosques in Monrovia, and nearly one hundred others in the rest of the country.

Asian immigrants in Liberia tend to practice Hinduism or Buddhism. There are nearly ten thousand Liberians who are of the Baha'i faith, a faith that honors many divine prophets, such as Moses, Jesus, Muhammad, Buddha, and Krishna. Liberia has proven to be a country where people of different religions coexist peacefully.

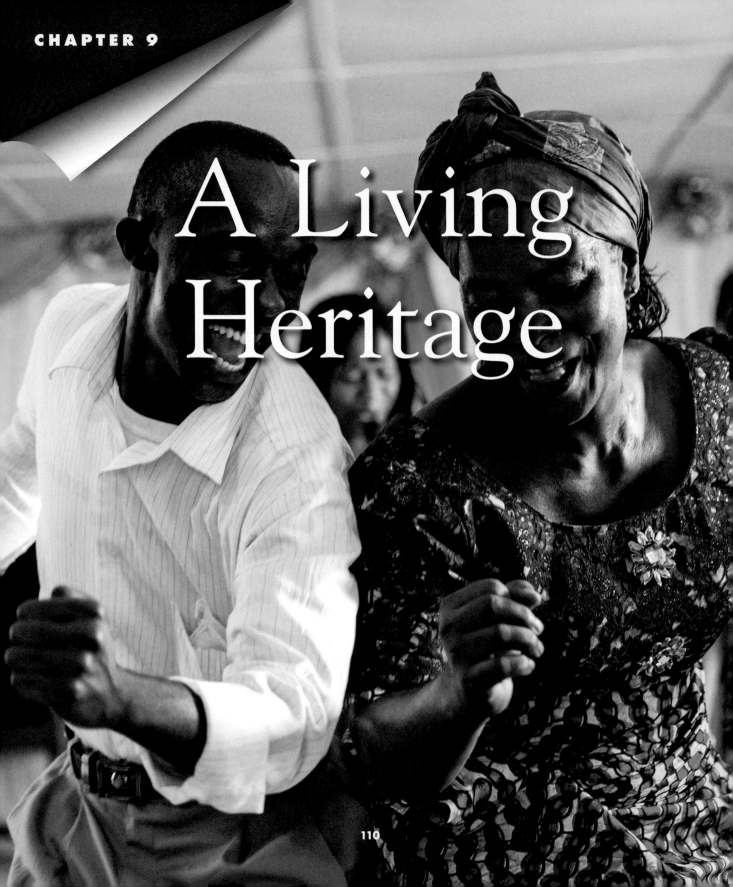

CHAPTER 9

A Living Heritage

LIBERIA HAS A VIBRANT CULTURAL HERITAGE THAT has endured across the years. Beauty and creativity can be found in every community. Liberians value their artists. When elders or parents recognize a special ability in a young child, whether it be wood carving, weaving, dancing, singing, or painting, they single the child out and everyone joins in to nourish and develop the child's talents. According to Won-Ldy Paye, a Liberian author and entertainer, "Liberian art, music, dance, and storytelling are a lifestyle."

Music

Music is part of everyday life and occasions both major and minor in Liberia. Whether at a wedding, greeting visitors, at worship, in the marketplace, at work at harvesttime, or simply at a casual gathering of friends and family, people are singing and dancing. Indigenous music is lively and rhythmic. Instruments are hand-made with great expertise. Besides the talking drum, musicians play rapid dance rhythms on a *keleng*, a hollowed-out log that is slit and played with sticks. Other Liberian instruments include

Opposite: **Dance is a central part of Liberian culture.**

Liberian men play sangbans, traditional drums of Liberia.

the *sangban*, a goblet drum made from a hollowed-out tree trunk and animal hide that is played by hand; the *dundun*, a bass drum also made from a hollowed-out tree trunk and hide that is played with sticks; and the *balafon*, a xylophone made from hardwood and played with mallets. The women's talking instrument is called the *saasaa*. It is a rattle made from a gourd with a long beaded net. Epic storytellers called griots accompany themselves on harp-like string instruments as they recount history.

Singing, chanting, and choral music are common in Liberia. Women are known for their singing groups that feature intricate vocal parts. The unique sound of Liberian indigenous music has influenced modern music throughout the world. Likewise, modern Liberian musicians draw from other global pop forms, such as gospel, American rhythm and blues, hip-hop, jazz, and musical styles from South America, the Caribbean, and other African countries.

Dance

Liberian dance is noted for its energy and passion and is part of everyone's life. Dance styles vary from village to village, with some of the best-known ones being performed by Mende, Vai, Kpelle, and Bassa dancers. The finest dancers are selected for dance troupes.

Many dancers, especially young girls, learn while taking part in their secret society initiation. Traditional dances tell stories or communicate with the spirits. Some dances are powerful and explosive, while others are more precise and graceful. Masks are an important part of traditional dances. Besides disguising the dancer's face, masks link dancers to secret societies, spirits, and ancestors. The Sowei mask, accompanied by a black raffia (grass) costume, is used in the girls' secret society and is one of the few female masks used in Africa. Contemporary dancers both in Liberia and throughout the world draw inspiration from the forms of traditional Liberian dance.

Arts and Crafts

West African arts and crafts are prized by Liberians and art collectors around the world. Liberian craftspeople are trained by their elders from youth to master design skills. Craftspeople decorate even everyday items, such as knives, pots, and baskets. The Mende make colorful fabrics with wax prints or tie-dye designs that are sold throughout western Africa. They are also known for their metalwork of gold and silver necklaces, bracelets, armlets, and earrings. Blacksmiths have always held a place of honor in communities because they are

responsible for making necessary household utensils, hunting knives, farm tools, and weapons.

Gola wood-carvers are known for their skill. Although today they make furniture or storage chests, in the past they were master mask makers. Because people believed that masks belonged to the spirit world, mask makers were considered to be part human, part spirit. Mask makers stayed hidden from view when they carved. The women who brought them food were not allowed to glimpse them at their work. The Loma were also known for their masks, which were made from long, hollowed-out tree trunks and carved into images of humans and animals.

Literature

The Vai and Bassa people had developed their own alphabet and written texts long before the American emigrants brought the English language to the country. While some literature in their native languages exists, the country is now formally educating more and more of its children in English, so English language books are becoming more available. The first novel written by an African and published in English was by Liberian author Joseph Walters in 1891. Since then, Liberia has been home to poets, novelists, short story writers, and playwrights. Many modern writers have left Liberia to go to school or flee the wars, and they have not returned. From afar, they write of their homeland. Helene Cooper, today a journalist for the *New York Times*, was born to a wealthy Americo-Liberian family and lived near Monrovia on Sugar Beach. After Samuel Doe assassinated President Tolbert, many wealthy people were hunted down and murdered. The Cooper family fled to the United States, and Doe's soldiers took over the family home. Cooper writes of the experience in her book *The House at Sugar Beach*. Bai T. Moore, a Gola novelist and poet who belonged to the Gola ethnic group, was a minister of culture who lived through the civil wars and wrote of his love for Liberia.

> **An Elder's Prayer**
>
> By Bai T. Moore
> Oh Great Spirit of the forest,
> I have nothing in my hand
> But a chicken and some rice
> It's the gift of all our land
> Bring us sunshine with the rain
> So the harvest moon may blow
> Save my people from all pains;
> When the harvest time is done
> We will make a feast to you.

Museums

Liberia, for all its culture, has few places where art is on display. Monrovia has many galleries and small museums, but war and poverty have greatly reduced their numbers. The National Museum of Liberia in Monrovia was once home to historic objects and documents, artifacts, traditional crafts, and contemporary African art. Now it is mostly destroyed from looting, though progress is being made to restore the building and collect old and new artifacts. Some masks and pottery were rescued and are now on display at Cuttington University. The Tubman Center of African Culture in Robertsport was a grand mansion that housed archaeological and ethnic artifacts. It, too, was looted and is still in ruins. However, outside the Liberia Broadcasting System in Paynesville stands a bronze sculpture of African dancers and a talking drum, symbolizing the rich traditions of Liberia that live on despite hardship.

Sports

Young people in Liberia enjoy playing soccer, called football in Liberia, as well as basketball and baseball. Other popular

The oldest Liberian flag was once on display at the National Museum of Liberia. Since the looting during the civil wars, however, it has been kept in an office.

sports are squash, surfing, kickball, tennis, and swimming. Most high schools, colleges, and many villages have a soccer team. Many Liberian officials believe that sports can help unify young people. Each year, Liberia holds a grand meet, where soccer players from all the counties compete and work out their ethnic rivalries on a sports field.

Liberia also has national soccer and basketball teams. The national soccer team, called the Lone Star, competes in international events. One of Liberia's greatest heroes is George Weah, a football player who in 1995 won the World Player of the Year award, the African Player of the Year award, the European Player of the Year award, and the African Player of the Century award. Weah is also an antiwar activist who ran for president. He sponsors many children's sports programs in Liberia and is President Johnson Sirleaf's peace ambassador.

George Weah (in blue) played professional soccer in Europe for fourteen years. A powerful and creative goal scorer, he is considered one of the greatest soccer players of all time.

CHAPTER 10

Family and Community

FAMILY LIFE IS THE CORE OF LIBERIAN SOCIETY. MOST Liberian families are made up of more than a mother and a father. Close families also include grandparents, aunts, uncles, and cousins as well as in-laws, second cousins, parents of cousins, and other more distant relatives. Beyond family, people also feel connected to clans, which are made up of groups of extended families.

Families treasure their children. Every child is welcomed to the village in a joyful celebration called the Naming Ceremony. On this day, elders, family members, and villagers select the name of the baby. The name is carefully chosen, as it reflects the baby's place in society. There is much feasting, music, and dancing. The African proverb "It takes a village to raise a child" is true in Liberian society.

Opposite: **A mother and child in Greenville, along Liberia's southern coast. On average, Liberian women have about five children.**

Farming is a traditional occupation for many Liberians.

Babies and young children are treated with care the first few years of their lives, but soon they are expected to help with chores. Children as young as three or four help with gathering firewood, fruits, and berries. Older siblings are expected to care for younger children. Around age six, many parents send their children to live with other relatives. There are several reasons for this, such as other families may be better able to send the children to school, or another family member possesses a skill that parents would like their children to learn.

Children have roles to play in helping their families earn a living. Many children raise chickens, tend cows, weed gardens, or help harvest crops. In marketplaces, children are often on hand to help their parents sell their products. Shopkeepers' children also have many tasks. Children are proud of their work and the help they provide their families.

Many workers follow traditional family occupations. That includes being farmers, fishers, merchants, village leaders, healers, teachers, laborers, construction workers, craftspeople, businesspeople, and government workers. Most Liberians are farmers, and the work is done with traditional tools. Children help by hoeing, planting, and weeding. Generally all villagers join in to harvest the crops. Some villagers are hunters and fishers. Fishers paddle boats in the lakes and use motorized dugout canoes along the Atlantic coast. In rivers, they stand on scaffolds and catch fish with nets and woven baskets. Most hunters use guns to kill game.

The Marketplace

Market day is a big, colorful, and lively event. Merchants set up stalls; some are lucky to have covers for their stalls in case it rains. Mostly women run the stalls selling foods, fish, meat, spices, clothing, baskets, weaving, dry goods, and school supplies. Men also work in the marketplace. They bring wheelbarrows filled with their wares and sell musical instruments, tools, and wood and metal crafts. Cities have large markets that are often open every day except Sunday.

Food

Liberia's climate provides the people with a bounty of food choices. The major staples are rice, palm oil, cassava, peppers, bananas, coconuts, yams, corn, vegetables, and leafy greens. People enjoy chicken, beef, goat, fish, and wild game. Some favorite meals are *dumboy*, a dumpling made from cassava squash; *fufu*, a doughy bread made from dried rice, plantains, or yams; beef stew; groundnut stew (peanuts); and chicken *jollof* rice, a spicy mixture of chicken, peppers, tomatoes, ginger, and rice. Women and girls do the family cooking. Most people cook on open fires, as electricity is rare.

Dress

Liberians love color and style. Clothes are made from colorful patterned cotton or linen fabrics. In cities and towns, many people dress in Western styles, either in business attire or in jeans, shorts, and shirts. However, many people, especially

A Liberian woman cooks a meal over an open fire.

Rice Bread

Liberians enjoy rice bread as a tasty treat on special occasions. Have an adult help you with this recipe.

Ingredients

2 cups rice, cooked and mashed

1½ bananas, mashed

3 tablespoons sugar

4 teaspoons baking powder

½ teaspoon salt

2 eggs

1½ cups milk

1 cup oil

Directions

Cook the rice according to the directions on the package. Mash the bananas and set them aside. In another bowl, mix together the rice, sugar, baking powder, and salt. Mix in the bananas, eggs, milk, and oil. Pour the mixture into a greased 9- by 12-inch pan and cook at 375°F for 45 minutes. Enjoy!

rural people, wear traditional clothing. Women wear a long wrapped skirt called a *lapa* and a loose top called a *bubba*. They also wear a headtie, called a *boubou*, which matches the rest of the outfit. Women wear their hair in elaborate braids or other fashionable hairdos. Traditional men's clothing includes pants or shorts and a loose, round-necked shirt called a *via*. A more formal outfit for men is a long tunic called an *abada*, and a round brimless hat.

Housing

Housing is simple in Liberia. Monrovia and other cities have some modern buildings, but there are many city dwellings of poor quality. People build their houses out of concrete block with grass or tin roofs. In the country, many people build mud huts with thatched roofs made from straw or reeds. Often, homes are just one or two rooms. Kitchens are outside, as are most latrines. Bright colors are popular in Liberia, so no matter how humble houses are, they are brightly painted or have murals on the walls. In most villages, houses are built right next to each other as a compound in a courtyard. Most villages have an open-air palava hut where ceremonies and village gatherings are held.

Health

Access to health care is very limited in Liberia. Monrovia has two major hospitals. Most of the few modern health clinics elsewhere are run by missionaries and aid organizations. Liberia's climate is a host to numerous contagious and sometimes deadly diseases carried by bats, insects, and other wild animals. If a villager becomes ill, it is difficult to get to a clinic or hospital. Roads are too rugged to travel and few people have vehicles, so many people rely on village healers.

In 2014, the deadly Ebola virus killed thousands of Liberians. Health care workers from around the world came to help the people. Foreign governments and missions quickly built new clinics in rural areas. It is hoped that the clinics will continue to operate and be staffed by newly trained Liberian medical workers.

A mother and child sit by their home in southern Liberia. The house has a roof made of palm fronds.

National Holidays

New Year's Day	January 1
Armed Forces Day	February 11
National Decoration Day	March 12
President J. J. Roberts' Birthday	March 15
Fast and Prayer Day	April
National Unification Day	May 14
Independence Day	July 26
Flag Day	August 24
Thanksgiving Day	November
President Tubman's Day (Goodwill Day)	November 29
Christmas Day	December 25

Ceremonies

Many ceremonies in Liberia celebrate daily life. There are naming ceremonies, secret society rituals, harvest rituals, marriages, and funerals. At each, there is feasting, dancing, chanting, drumming, and music. Most ceremonies are led by a village leader, often a woman. Liberia has celebrations in common with the United States, such as Christmas, Easter, and Thanksgiving. Other celebrations include, Fast and Prayer Day, President Tubman's Day (also called Goodwill Day), Flag Day, and Independence Day.

Liberians are known to be friendly and kind. They are close to their families, loyal to their friends, and hospitable to strangers. They share whatever they have and would not deny anyone food, water, or shelter. Liberians honor their elders and respect their leaders. Their society is strong despite the enormous challenges they have faced. The Liberian people have proven their strength and resilience. They are a nation of survivors. As the Liberian proverb says, "The elephant never gets tired of carrying its tusks."

A Wedding Celebration

Marriage is extremely important to Liberians. Not only do husband and wife join together, but their entire families also become united. Liberians have huge families and many friends, so Liberian weddings are large. Some Liberian weddings are modeled after Western weddings, with bridesmaids, best men, limousines, wedding cakes, and flowers. But many Liberians celebrate their weddings in traditional ways.

Bridesmaids, of which there are many, wear colorful skirts and blouses adorned with intricate embroidery, and matching head wraps. Best men wear long pants and shirts under a long robe, with a matching small hat. The bride and the groom dress similarly to the maids of honor and the groomsmen, but their garments are white with gold stitching.

Traditionally, parents of the bride and the groom perform a ceremony where the groom's family pays a bride price, or dowry, to the bride's family to show their appreciation for the sacrifices they made in raising their daughter. The bride's family offers drinks and gifts to the groom's parents. The ceremony is accompanied by traditional singing and dancing.

The celebration of the wedding is a large feast. Family and friends prepare the food, which includes soup, rice dishes, cassava leaves, baked fish, meatballs, fresh fruit, and rice bread. A cow is traditionally butchered, cooked, and served. The wedding day is filled with special dances, songs, and blessings.

Timeline

LIBERIAN HISTORY		WORLD HISTORY	
		ca. 2500 BCE	The Egyptians build the pyramids and the Sphinx in Giza.
		ca. 563 BCE	The Buddha is born in India.
		313 CE	The Roman emperor Constantine legalizes Christianity.
		610	The Prophet Muhammad begins preaching a new religion called Islam.
Arab traders arrive in the region.	ca. 750		
		1054	The Eastern (Orthodox) and Western (Roman Catholic) Churches break apart.
		1095	The Crusades begin.
Sixteen ethnic groups of Liberia migrate to the region.	11th–17th centuries	1215	King John seals the Magna Carta.
		1300s	The Renaissance begins in Italy.
		1347	The plague sweeps through Europe.
		1453	Ottoman Turks capture Constantinople, conquering the Byzantine Empire.
Portuguese explorer Pedro de Sintra arrives in what is now Liberia.	1461	1492	Columbus arrives in North America.
Trade expands between West Africa and Europe; the slave trade becomes highly profitable.	1500s	1500s	Reformers break away from the Catholic Church, and Protestantism is born.
		1776	The U.S. Declaration of Independence is signed.
		1789	The French Revolution begins.
Great Britain ends its slave trade.	1808		
The American Colonization Society is formed.	1816		

LIBERIAN HISTORY

The first group of freed black Americans arrive in what is now Monrovia.	**1822**
Liberia becomes an independent nation.	**1847**
Firestone establishes a rubber plantation in Liberia.	**1926**
William V. S. Tubman begins twenty-seven years as president.	**1944**
Samuel Kanyon Doe leads a takeover of the government.	**1980**
Charles Taylor leads rebel soldiers in a civil war against Doe's government.	**1989**
Charles Taylor is elected president.	**1997**
A second civil war begins.	**1999**
Ellen Johnson Sirleaf becomes the first woman in Africa to be elected president.	**2005**
Thousands die in an Ebola outbreak.	**2014**

WORLD HISTORY

1865	The American Civil War ends.
1879	The first practical lightbulb is invented.
1914	World War I begins.
1917	The Bolshevik Revolution brings communism to Russia.
1929	A worldwide economic depression begins.
1939	World War II begins.
1945	World War II ends.
1969	Humans land on the Moon.
1975	The Vietnam War ends.
1989	The Berlin Wall is torn down as communism crumbles in Eastern Europe.
1991	The Soviet Union breaks into separate states.
2001	Terrorists attack the World Trade Center in New York City and the Pentagon near Washington, D.C.
2004	A tsunami in the Indian Ocean destroys coastlines in Africa, India, and Southeast Asia.
2008	The United States elects its first African American president.

Fast Facts

Official name: Republic of Liberia

Capital: Monrovia

Official language: English

Monrovia

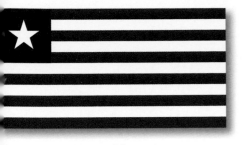

National flag

Official religion: None

Year of founding: 1847

National anthem: "All Hail, Liberia, Hail!"

Type of government: Democracy

Head of state: President

Head of government: President

Area of country: 38,250 square miles (99,067 sq km)

Latitude and longitude of geographic center: 6° N, 10° W

Bordering countries: Sierra Leone to the northwest, Guinea to the northeast, Côte d'Ivoire to the east

Highest elevation: Mount Wuteve, 4,724 feet (1,440 m) above sea level

Lowest elevation: Sea level along the coast

Longest river: Cavalla, 320 miles (515 km)

Average high temperature: In Monrovia, 88°F (31°C) in January, 84°F (29°C) in July

Average low temperature: In Monrovia, 70°F (21°C) in January, 70°F (21°C) in July

Average ocean temperature: 81°F (27°C)

Average annual precipitation: 202 inches (514 cm) in Monrovia

Coastline

Kpatawee Falls

National population
(2013 est.): 4,294,077

Population of major
cities (2008 est.):

Monrovia	1,021,762
Gbanga	333,481
Buchanan	50,245
Zwedru	25,349
Harbel	25,309

Landmarks:
- ▶ *Kpatawee Falls*, Gbanga
- ▶ *Mount Wuteve*, Wologizi Range
- ▶ *National Museum of Liberia*, Monrovia
- ▶ *Robertsport*, Cape Mount
- ▶ *Sapo National Park*, Grand Gedeh County

Economy: The principal industry is agriculture, and major products include rubber, palm oil, coconuts, and rice. Farmers also raise goats, cattle, and chickens. Timber is an important industry. Iron, gold, and diamonds are mined and exported. The Freeport of Monrovia is an important international harbor.

Currency: The Liberian dollar. In 2015, L$92 equaled US$1.

System of weights
and measures: Both U.S. customary units and metric measurements are used

Literacy rate (2015): 48%

Currency

Schoolgirl

George Weah

Liberian English words and phrases:

bug-a-bug	crazy
chunk	to throw
cold water	a peace offering
country chop	indigenous food
dress	excuse me
griot	traditional storyteller
money bus	pickup truck converted with wooden bench seats used as public transportation
palava hut	public meeting place in center of village used for courts, ceremonies, and public meetings

Prominent Liberians:

Leymah Gbowee (1972–)
Nobel Peace Prize winner

Ellen Johnson Sirleaf (1938–)
President

Bai T. Moore (1916–1988)
Poet and novelist

Joseph Jenkins Roberts (1809–1876)
President

George Weah (1966–)
Soccer player

To Find Out More

Books

▶ Barr, Gary. *History and Activities of the West African Kingdoms.* Chicago: Heinemann Library, 2007.

▶ Reese, Katherine E. *West African Kingdoms.* New York: Marshall Cavendish Benchmark, 2010.

▶ Stone, Ruth M. *Music in West Africa: Experiencing Music, Expressing Culture.* New York: Oxford University Press, 2005.

▶ Streissguth, Thomas. *Liberia in Pictures.* Vero Beach, FL: Rourke, 2006.

Music

▶ *Folk Music of Liberia.* Washington, DC: Smithsonian Folkways, 2012.

▶ *Suku: The Music of Vai Islam.* Music of the Earth, 2007.

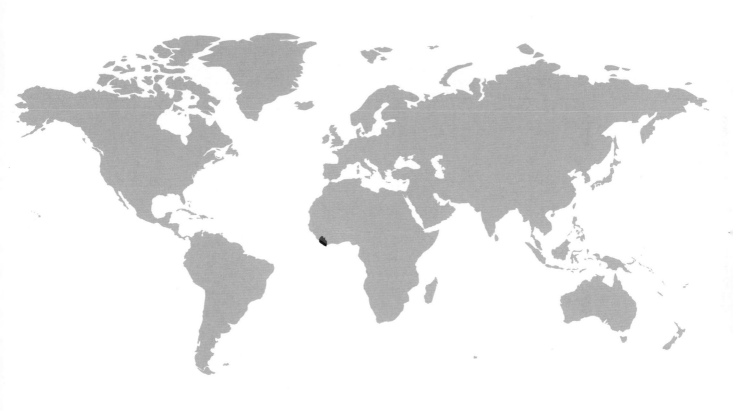

▶ Visit this Scholastic Web site for more information on Liberia:
www.factsfornow.scholastic.com
Enter the keyword Liberia

Index

Page numbers in *italics* indicate illustrations.

Meet the Author

RUTH BJORKLUND SPENT HER CHILDHOOD IN RURAL New England, living in a house on a lake where she developed a love of nature and a passion for living near water. She spent summers rowing her small boat and hiking in the nearby woods. When she was twenty, she packed up her belongings and moved to the Pacific Northwest.

She graduated from the University of Washington with a degree in comparative literature and later earned a master's degree in library and information science. She worked for several years as a children's and young adult librarian and then began writing books for young people. She has written on a variety of subjects, including Ancient China, Afghanistan, wildlife, immigration, and alternative energy.

Bjorklund presently lives on Bainbridge Island, a ferry ride away from Seattle, Washington, and is building a small home in Baja California, Mexico. From her home in the Northwest, she has traveled to Thailand, China, Kyrgyzstan, Indonesia, Mexico, Italy, Croatia, and Peru. Wherever and whenever she can, she enjoys sailing, snorkeling, birding, kayaking, fly-fishing, and at the end of the day, a comfortable place to read.

Photo Credits